ABOUT THE AUTHORS

David Smith joined Reuters from Oxford and was a correspondent for them in Spain and Italy before moving to Independent Television News (ITN) in 1978. For ITN he has worked widely in Africa. In 1979 he covered the Lancaster House conference on Rhodesia and then, from Salisbury, the subsequent ceasefire and election which brought Mugabe to power. He and his American wife, Pam, live in London.

Ian Davies who has worked for the *Sunday Times* Insight team is now with the *Melbourne Age*.

Colin Simpson has been a special correspondent of the *Sunday Times* since 1964. He uncovered the Rhodesian sanctions scandal of 1969 and is the author of several best sellers including *Lusitania, Lawrence of Arabia* and, most recently, *The Ship That Hunted Itself.*

D0869564

Mugabe

**DAVID SMITH and COLIN SIMPSON
with IAN DAVIES**

SPHERE BOOKS LIMITED
30–32 Gray's Inn Road, London WC1X 8JL

First published in Great Britain by Sphere Books Ltd 1981
Copyright © David Smith, Colin Simpson,
Ian Davies 1981

TRADE
MARK

Set in Monophoto Times

Printed and bound in Great Britain by
©ollins, Glasgow

CONTENTS

ACKNOWLEDGEMENTS

Robert Mugabe is a retiring man. We are grateful
to the following persons who – each after their
fashion – have enabled us to find and follow his
footsteps. They are: Mr Nathan Shamuyarira,
Mr Godwin Matatu, Mr Lawrence Vambe,
Mr Marrin Meredith, Ms Heidi Holland, Ms Ruth
Weiss, Ms Judy Todd, Father Trabers, Ms Jenny
Barraclough, Sister Janice McLaughlin, Lord
Soames and his staff, Mr David Martin, Mr Colin
Legum, Mr Neal Acherson, Mr Guy Clutton-
Brock, Mr Robert Blake, Mr Dennis Hills,
Ms Elaine Windrich, Professor Terence Ranger,
the Reverend Bill Clark, Ms Ida Grant, Senator
Andrew Young, Mr Mike Aurett, Superintendent
Tony Bradshaw, Mr Walter Kamba and
Lord and Lady Walston. We have a special debt
to Ms Sally Mugabe for being allowed to use
her reminiscences, to Mr and Mrs Boohene of
Ghana, Mr Eric Marsden, Mr Garfield Todd,
and from our immediate colleagues at the *Sunday
Times* and ITN. In particular *Sunday Times*
editor, Mr Harold Evans, who allowed us access
to the archives of Times Newspapers; Mr John
Barry, the managing editor who organised the
Sunday Times coverage of the Zimbabwe
Settlement Crisis; David Nicholas, the editor of

ITN, and Mr Tony Millett and Mr John Flewin of ITN for their encouragement and help. And special thanks to Simon Freeman of the *Sunday Times* without whom the book would not have been possible. Lastly, three women have been invaluable: Mr Mugabe's mother who granted us a rare and valuable tape recorded interview at Kutama Mission, and our respective wives, Jane Simpson who organised the research and Pamela Smith who took all the strain when a deadline had to be met.

MUGABE

Chapter 1 — Finding Himself

In the rainy season, there could hardly be a more forsaken place on earth.

When the rains came, there was only one way to it from the desolate railway station eight miles away. On foot, through deep bush and tall elephant grass, where lions were said to prey. It was only 50 miles from Salisbury but it belonged to another world and another age.

At the end of a walk that could take half a day stood a Gothic-style church, a primitive clinic and a collection of damp mud huts.

This was Kutama – literal meaning 'to migrate' – named after the local African chief who in the years before the first World War had converted both himself and his people to Christianity. In return, the Jesuits built a mission station, an elementary school and a teacher training college that was to become renowned throughout Rhodesia and Africa for the men and women it produced.

The Jesuits were sticklers for ceremony, be it daily mass, weekly confession or the monthly review of a pupil's progress. For the boys and girls who made it through elementary school, the fathers had devised a special passing-out ceremony. It was the final day of school, and for most of them education would end there. Each pupil was asked to appear on the makeshift wooden platform that was the school stage and announce to their teachers and parents what they were going to do with their lives. They walked into the centre of the stage and completed the couplet:

'When I am a man, I'll be a ... if I can.'

Some came on with the cape and stick of the herdsman,

others with the hammer and saw of the carpenter, or the axe of the woodsman. This day one little boy appeared in gown and mortar board, surreptitiously borrowed from the mission father. As the audience gave way to a collective chuckle, he walked proudly to the middle of the stage, took a deep breath and declared:

'When I am a man, I'll be a teacher if I can.'

The year was 1938. The boy was Robert Gabriel Mugabe.

It was said by some that the founder of the mission, a Frenchman called Jean-Baptiste Loubiere, had been transferred to Rhodesia at the beginning of the Great War because he had fallen in love with a girl at his previous post, in Portuguese East Africa. If so, he made up for his 'falling' in the eyes of the Jesuits with his work at Kutama.

The regime of Father Loubiere and his African assistant, Joseph Dambaza, assumed an almost monastic rigidity. There was little room for African customs, let alone tribal religion. They were both convinced that their mission in life was to send as many black souls to heaven as possible. To achieve that Father Loubiere ordered the tribespeople to look upon the world outside as a pit of evil which could only be redeemed through their constant prayer. Lawrence Vambe, the distinguished Rhodesian historian, has compared the atmosphere at Kutama in its early days to that of Lourdes at the time of a pilgrimage. The village's patron saint was Theresa of Lisieux, the Little Flower. So intense was the devotion to her that the villagers substituted her name for the Virgin Mary in some of their prayers.

If in the years to come, the most famous son of Kutama was to insist on 'Africanisation' of his people, it was perhaps because his tribe had had its African way of life so effectively wiped out at the mission. Father Loubiere even made the women wear high-necked, ankle-length dresses covering every inch of their bodies. Their spirit mediums – the wise men who represented the wishes of ancestral spirits and were sought for spiritual guidance and blessing in times of war – were either converted or outlawed. From the moment the mission was built, every task of the day was accompanied by prayer and exhortation for the redemption of mankind in general – and that of the local inhabitants in particular.

One man found the atmosphere too stifling. That was Gabriel Mugabe, the mission carpenter. He opted for the more informal life of a travelling craftsman and in 1934 left the mission and his family for a jobbing carpenter's position in Bulawayo, and then the mines in South Africa. He did not return. It was said, to the chagrin of the missionaries, that he took a second wife. Rarely, if ever, did he contribute to the family he left behind. The family were one of the most devout in the village. There was his wife Bona, a formidable woman imbued with a Christianity that mixed intensity with piety, and her four children: Miteri (Michael), the eldest, Raphael, Robert Gabriel, Dhonandho (Donald), and the youngest, Sabina. The year their father left, Michael died in tragic and somewhat mysterious circumstances from eating poisoned maize.

The three boys left all had a traditional, active African upbringing, learning to fend for themselves and make money for the rest of the family as quickly as they could. They helped tend the cattle of their mother's father, they fished in the river, and very occasionally they would be allowed to play in the forest near the misty swamp that was infested by the anophelene mosquito, the carrier of a deadly malaria. Even on its good days, the smell of quinine hung over this sad settlement.

The young Mugabe absorbed the monasticism of the mission without losing his sense of proportion. On more than one occasion he eschewed, in front of his family and friends, the more extreme teachings of the mission

11

fathers. He didn't like the idea, fostered by Father Loubiere, of calling the white materialist man of the cities 'mboga' – mispronunciation of the Shona word 'dog' – and he said so.

In 1930 Father Loubiere died and was succeeded by a remarkable Irish priest called Father O'Hea, who set out to reverse the 'spell' cast by his predecessor and bring Kutama into the twentieth century.

Father O'Hea revolutionised the place and its people. Devoting his substantial private means to the mission under his care, he founded a teacher training school to supplement the primary education already there. Then he added a technical college as well. The white government in Salisbury tried to block him. They actively discouraged any higher education for the African. When the government refused to help him build a hospital, he went ahead and did it with his own money. His contempt and spirit of rebellion against the whites found a young disciple in Mugabe. In return, Father O'Hea carefully nurtured the young boy. He recognised already what, shortly before his death in 1970, he was to call 'an exceptional mind and an exceptional heart'.

Mugabe was only nine but he remembered one day more than almost any other from his childhood. It was 1933 and the newly elected prime minister, Geoffrey Huggins, came to inspect Kutama. He brought his high commissioner from London, a Mr O'Keefe.

Because he wanted to raise money for his mission, Father O'Hea also persuaded the governor, Cecil Rodwell, to come too. Kutama had never had a day like it before. It has had one since. Mugabe, as Prime Minister, returned to Kutama in triumph in June 1980.

The school put on a display for the distinguished visitors. The choir sang. There was even meat for lunch. Father O'Hea was lobbying for money for that hospital. The Africans in the area – it was 10,000 square miles – did not even have a clinic or a dispensary.

12

Governor Rodwell remarked: 'Why do you worry about a hospital – after all there are too many natives in the country already.'

Father O'Hea never forgave or forgot that comment. Neither did Mugabwe.

The hospital came, anyway, and it made Kutama the centre for everyone in the vast Zwimba reserve. The priest himself doubled up as a doctor and would work round the clock to take care of the sick. That left him little or no time for his spiritual duties and it wasn't long before the fierce religious discipline of Father Louviere began to disappear. The men took to drink, violence returned as a way of life; the people went back to indolent self-destruction. The young Mugabe never forgot that either.

Even in Father Loubiere's day, the mission had received daily newspapers from Salisbury which African students were encouraged to read. Now, such was the style of Father O'Hea's mission, the boys would gather outside his office in the evenings to listen to the world news on his wireless. Who was Hitler, they would ask? Why had Mussolini invaded Abyssinia? Furthermore, why did the Pope bless the Italian soldiers going to Abysinnia, as the picture in the paper showed? And how long would it take Generalissimo Franco (as Catholics they supported the Nationalists) to win the war in Spain?

Father O'Hea would explain patiently to them what was going on, never leaving them in any doubt about what he thought of Hitler and Mussolini. The smallest boy in the group would stand at the back and say little, except that he didn't like Hitler.

Mugabe, at this stage, was very much the youngest and the smallest among older contemporaries. Within a couple of years of arriving at Kutama, Father O'Hea had noticed the boy and marked him down in his own mind. There was not just his hunger to learn in class; or his devotion to his mother, with whom he always came to church. There was, above all, his seriousness, his 'unusual gravitas' as Father O'Hea put it. He rushed Mugabe ahead, far quicker than almost any other pupil. 'We all knew him as a very clever lad,' recalls David Garwe, now a headmaster himself and then a friend of Mugabe's. 'He was by far the youngest boy in his class. Though he was three years younger than me, he was only one class below.

'I suppose the fact that he was younger and smaller may have kept him a little apart from everyone. I don't remember him taking part in sport or school plays. He always seemed to enjoy his own company.'

The six grades of elementary education over, Father O'Hea offered Mugabe a course in the teacher training school. The boy himself wanted to, it was a decision he had made several years before. But there was pressure from his family for him to take his father's place, learn a trade or become a farmer, to support his mother and his brothers and sisters. A course in teacher training would prove a heavy strain on the family's slender resources. His mother's only income came from teaching the village girls their catechism.

It was typical of his mother's faith that when Father O'Hea told her just how much he wanted Robert to go ahead and train as a teacher, she agreed immediately. Whatever the cost to the family, Robert would go. As it was, Father O'Hea himself provided a bursary for him from his own income: the other money came from Mugabe's farmer–grandfather. Robert had seen the problems ahead when he had publicly opted for teaching in the passing-out ceremony: 'if I can'. Now they had been resolved.

Years later, Father O'Hea said: 'I would have kept him for nothing because of his influence over the other boys. Before long he was teaching his classmates how to teach.'

For the next two years, Mugabe was to learn a lot more than just the ability to teach. For the first time he

14

began to form his own ideas, taking from the Jesuits and moulding them after his own fashion. Today he will say: 'I was brought up by the Jesuits and I'm most grateful ... I benefitted from their teaching enormously.' That rather hides the manner in which his socialism took roots in Kutama.

Men like Father O'Hea did not preach the 'Hell and Damnation' of their predecessors. Theirs was a far more tolerant Christianity, they aimed to make their African communities 'Christian' in thought and deed.

Father O'Hea would even tell his villagers not to come to Mass if it did not mean anything to them, the kind of progressive thinking that Loubiere would never have countenanced.

Furthermore, the mission at Kutama preached equality as a way of life at a time when the rest of Rhodesia – and for that matter Africa – was based on discrimination. The white fathers had made themselves part of the community, they enjoyed little privacy from the tribespeople who looked to them for almost everything – from food to medicine and education. Father O'Hea never stopped living out his own goal: to be 'one' with his people.

Slowly, Mugabe drew his own conclusions. From Loubiere, from Father O'Hea, from Geoffrey Huggins the day the prime minister came to visit, even from the man Hitler he heard about on the radio. At this stage of his life, he probably never heard of the word 'socialism'. But that was what he was aspiring to.

'To my way of thinking,' he has since recalled, religious communities, ancient and modern, are socialist. In its own way, Kutama was.

'Because of that, and ever since then, it has always been my firm belief that socialism has to be much more christian than capitalism.'

In the mid-1940s he graduated with a diploma in teaching. In 1945 he left Kutama – a serious young man, something of a loner, diligent, hard-working, a voracious reader who used every minute of his time, not much given to laughter: but, above all, single-minded.

A series of teaching jobs followed, all over the country. Rarely did the quiet, intense young man spend more than a couple of terms at one school. At one, Dadaya Mission school, he met Ndabaningi Sithole, already aspiring to nationalist politics. Mugabe had time only for study and his teaching. In 1949, when he was already 25, he won what he wanted: a scholarship to university.

It was to give him his political baptism and his first taste of African nationalism.

Fort Hare was an all-black university on the Cape in South Africa which during the 1940s had educated the new, young wing of the African National Congress (ANC) of South Africa. The movement itself was undergoing a vital change in style, moving from a policy of co-operation with the authorities to one of confrontation. The young lions of Fort Hare, as they were called, were largely responsible for the radical change in black thinking that the ANC was trying to instil among its people. By the time Mugabe arrived, men like Nelson Mandela, Robert Sobukwe (yet to become respectively heads of the ANC and the pan-African congress), the Zulu Bantustan leader Gatasha Buthelezi and aspiring ANC militants like Oliver Tambo dominated political life on the campus.

They were one influence, so too were the Jewish communists of South Africa who didn't study there but were noisy contributors to nationalist meetings. They introduced Mugabe to Marxism. 'I felt already that I was a revolutionary,' Mugabe says of his time there. The fact is that he was a long way from being that. He had merely been introduced to Marxism, he did not become a disciple until much later.

Mugabe was, at this stage, still very much a butterfly. Kutama had fostered socialism in his own mind. At Fort Hare there was the heady rhetoric of revolution from the

16

ANC, the dreams of black majority rule, the disgust at the condition of fellow Africans. There was also the hero-worship, among students there, of Mahatma Gandhi – whose campaign of 'passive resistance' in India made him a cult figure for young nationalists in South Africa (where Gandhi had been born and brought up).

As the butterfly emerging from a chrysalis, the sun which warmed and dried the young Mugabe's wings was not revolution, but the more cerebral attraction of non-violence as advocated by Ghandi.

Mugabe himself looks back on his years at Fort Hare as the 'turning-point' in his life. He had confirmed his opposition to everything the likes of Geoffrey Huggins stood for, indeed there was now open hostility to the whites in Rhodesia.

'When I left Fort Hare I had a new orientation and outlook,' Mugabe says. 'I came from a country where most black people had accepted European rule as such.

'Most of us believed that all that should be done was to remove our grievances within the system. After Fort Hare there was a radical change in my views.

'I was completely hostile ... but of course I came back to Rhodesia to teach within the system.'

With his Bachelor of Arts degree, he got a job at the Briefontein Mission near Umvuna. He had joined the ANC in his final days at Fort Hare, but politically he was to lie dormant when he got back home. He preferred to study for a further degree, a diploma in education. He'd moved on to a mission school in Gwelo by the time he got it.

There he met an old friend from Kutama, Leopold Takawira. Takawira had been training for the priesthood at the mission as Mugabe was going through school. Though several years older than him, he had befriended the boy Mugabe. Now he was teaching at the mission. He had given up the idea of the priesthood, recognising already that his future lay in politics.

17

Because Takawira died before Mugabe had really emerged as a nationalist leader, his influence on him has never been properly recognised. Takawira was a man of rare energy combined with the most attractive of personalities. He could condemn the racial injustice of his country bitterly: but he always balanced it with his belief in the good of man. He applied that to both his own people and the whites. He had left his seminary because he realised that the way to right the wrongs done to Africans was not through the Church. Redemption for the blacks did not mean saving their souls, but removing the laws of segregation and discrimination that made them helpless, pitiful victims of their own worst traits and the system.

To Mugabe, still searching for a philosophy and rather more keenly pursuing his education, Takawira was a political tutor. It was Takawira who first equated for Mugabe the relationship between simple Christianity – which he'd learned at Kutama – and the basic principles of Karl Marx, which he'd been introduced to at Fort Hare.

Now Mugabe was sending off to London, to a mail order firm, for copies of *Das Kapital*, even Engels' *Conditions of the Working Classes*. And now Mugabe started to attend meetings of inter-racial groups like the Capricorn Society.

The society had been founded by Colonel David Stirling, a hero of Britain's Second World War campaign in North Africa. Stirling had come to Rhodesia after the war, and was genuinely shocked by the 'false paradise' he said he found there. He set up the society as a means of bringing blacks and whites together. The hope was that, through discussion, a government of consent and the sharing of economic and political power might avoid the bloodshed that Stirling feared even in these early days. The colonel was to be disappointed. His plan demanded

18

that the Europeans face up to the truth he saw. They didn't.

A British couple, Guy and Molly Clutton-Brock, were heavily involved in these first attempts at racial conciliation. Guy used to hold discussion groups among African teachers. He remembers Mugabe from virtually the first meeting he attended, with Takawira.

'I was surprised at just how articulate he was, and how widely read,' he recalls. 'He neither drank nor smoked, in fact he could be a bit of a cold fish at times. But beneath it all there was an extraordinary young man, almost reluctant to emerge from beneath his self-imposed shell.

'He had this wide range of interests, he could talk about Elvis Presley or Bing Crosby as easily as politics. Above all he had an overwhelming thirst for knowledge.'

It was at one of Guy Clutton-Brock's meetings, at a mission near Rusape, that retired teacher Alfred Knottenbelt met Mugabe and formed a lasting impression of him. Knottenbelt had taught in South Africa, one of his pupils had been Robert Sobukwe. He was something of a judge of young nationalists. 'Mugabe,' he says, 'joined in more than anyone else, he knew what he was talking about and he wasn't frightened to take over the discussion.'

'We didn't talk politics directly – it was taboo in those days – but you could tell that here was a chap with a clear vision of what the blacks needed to progress.'

If Mugabe couldn't talk politics there, he did occasionally in his classroom. During this period, the early 1950s, he was always taking newspaper clips about the Kenyan nationalist Jomo Kenyatta and the Mau-Mau into his lessons. He would tell his pupils that what was happening in Kenya was bound, sooner or later, to happen in Rhodesia.

Still, for his friends like Takawira, he remained something of an enigma: a nationalist in heart and mind, but not committed. Some, Takawira among them, argued that he was wasting his talents as a mission schoolteacher. They played devil's advocate to him. Why, they asked, is a man with your intellect, your qualifications and your beliefs burying himself in remote mission schools when you could be in the thick of young African idealism in Salisbury?

They teased him, suggesting that he was supporting and perpetuating the system he professed to despise. Mugabe would always reply that he was not ready. And that until he was, he was prepared to work within the system.

The fact was that Mugabe had little time for the militancy and hard line being taken by the champions of nationalism at that stage.

One of them he knew well. James Chikerema, a schoolmate from Kutama and the son of Loubiere's assistant Joseph Dambaza, was rapidly emerging as one of the leading lights of African protest in Salisbury. He was three years older than Mugabe and had gone to South Africa to study before him. There he had been deeply involved with the Communist party. In 1948 the South Africans had expelled him and he had returned to the Salisbury township of Harare to mobilise black support for his radical views. By now his Communism had developed into outright rejection of everything Kutama stood for. Chikerema's Marxist Leninism did not abide by the church.

Mugabe could not accept that, his embryonic Marxism was still compatible with his Christian beliefs. He may have endorsed Chikerema's aims – to strip the whites of their power and win black majority rule – but he could not support the means or the philosophy.

Partly to prevent himself becoming entangled with Chikerema, and partly because he wanted to earn more money, he moved to Zambia in 1955 to teach and study, this time for his third degree. He was more immersed in his reading than ever before and it seemed to all who met him then that he had opted for a lifetime of teaching and scholarship. With the few Rhodesians he talked politics to, he appeared to have buried any aspirations to a career as a nationalist.

Ghana, where he moved in the autumn of 1957, was to change all that, Mugabe is reticent about what prompted his move, but there is little doubt that it was by invitation.

Ghana was on the verge of independence, the first of Britain's colonies in Africa to achieve it. Kwame Nkrumah, the leader of the country's nationalists and shortly to be the first president, was inviting literate Africans from other countries to work, study and teach in his country. Not only did Nkrumah need all the talent he could find, he also realised that under his young revolution these men and women could discover the ways and means to bring their own countries to independence. All Africa would look to Ghana for their lead, Nkrumah hoped.

The example of Ghana fired the imagination of Mugabe and everyone who went with him. They were heady days, as one of Mugabe's Rhodesian colleagues there remembers.

'Ghanaians were just like the rest of us, but free. I remember my first visit, around the same time as Robert's.

'My first desire was just to set my eyes on an African prime minister and African ministers. When the first excitement wore off, it occurred to me that most of these men were no different to African friends of mine in Salisbury – but those friends were getting one-tenth of the opportunities available in Ghana.

'It wasn't just on the political level, either. Africans were being made directors of companies, headmasters of schools, heads of departments. I, like everyone else, went

21

back to Rhodesia determined to stop the whites blocking us in every sphere of life '

Mugabe revelled in this new environment. 'I went as an adventurist,' he says, 'I wanted to see what it would be like in an independent African state.

'Once there I began to develop definite ideas. You could say that it was there I accepted the general principles of Marxism.' Whether he alone would have turned his 'education' in Ghana into a political career in Rhodesia remains an open question. But then he met Sally Heyfron.

Sally was a teacher at St Mary's college in Takoradi, on the coast west of Accra, where Mugabe was first assigned. Hers was a middle-class family committed to teaching and community service. Her father was an agriculture teacher at the college, her mother a social worker, lay magistrate and professional seamstress. Sally and her twin sister Esther went to Achimota secondary school, one of Ghana's best, before Sally returned to St Mary's to teach.

The Heyfrons went out of their way to entertain and take care of the Africans Nkrumah had invited to teach in Ghana. So when Mugabe burned himself, badly enough to need treatment in hospital, Sally visited him regularly. It was not, friends say, love at first sight: rather an instant rapport that grew steadily the more time they spent together. Sally is as strong as she is unselfish. She has a toughness and serenity which is rare and which with hindsight, Mugabe recognised that he needed. Because over the years it has been Sally who has honed his political instincts into the complete politician Mugabe is today; Sally who has put the iron into his soul.

When pressed, she will say that she loves him for his kindness and his integrity as a man. Mugabe, tongue in cheek, tries to be infinitely more prosaic about it. 'I married a Ghanaian because Ghanaian women don't leave men to do all the work.'

Over the years Sally's family have come to know Mugabe in a way few others have. They first saw him as a young teacher, the very private man before he became a politician. When they have seen him since, it has been as an in-law; not as Mugabe the guerrilla leader, Mugabe the negotiator, Mugabe the prime minister.

Few men are heroes to their in-laws but Sally's family are disarmingly honest about their admiration for 'Bob', as they call him. Their insight into this most self-effacing of men has been reached over 20 years.

In March 1980, after Mugabe's election victory, we spoke to Sally's sister Esther and her husband Kojo Boohene. Mr Boohene could hardly be a sharper contrast to Mugabe. He's a businessman with interests in food processing and distribution throughout West Africa. Over the years, Mugabe the revolutionary and Boohene the business tycoon have become close friends.

'You see,' says Kojo Boohene, 'Bob is a very discerning man. The basis of his political outlook has been, and always will be, his care for the underdog. I share that but we disagree when it comes to deciding how to get a better lot for the underdog. For instance, I find the co-operative communes which Bob would like to set up in Zimbabwe inefficient. I am for getting the cake big, Bob is more interested in getting everyone involved in making the cake, which in the long run might produce a cake that's not so big.

'So we agree to disagree.'

Esther Boohene butted in. 'The most impressive thing about Bob is that he's very simple, and very sympathetic. If you say something he doesn't agree with, he won't use his great learning to make you look ridiculous. He will just point out where he thinks you are wrong. Even if you persist, he will still listen to you.' Would Mr Boohene, the capitalist, get out of Zimbabwe under Robert Mugabe if he were a businessman there?

23

'No, I would not. At the end of the day, Bob knows what is good, and you can trust him to discern the wheat from the chaff. If you've listened to him over the years, you would have noticed he's been doing it all along.

'Who would have thought that Bob, generally assumed to be the rank Marxist, would talk to Ian Smith, who has treated him like a dog? Who would have thought that Bob, the so-called arch terrorist, would be bringing whites into his government? He knows what to do. No one has anything to fear from him.'

By the end of 1960 Mugabe felt it was time to go home. He wanted Sally to meet his mother and family before they married.

They had made their minds up on that, but they had yet to decide whether they would live in Ghana or Rhodesia. Mugabe took leave for Christmas that year and together they travelled to Salisbury. It was, they said, just to be a holiday.

But in their hearts, they both knew that they were looking for the chance to join the nationalists and apply the Ghanaian example to Rhodesia.

They did not have long to wait.

Chapter 2 — The Struggle

It was 2.30 in the morning when the crowd, its numbers swelling all the time en route, reached the Stoddart Hall in the Salisbury township of Harare.

Up till now their spirits had been good. They danced, they sang, they chanted slogans of the National Democratic Party (NDP), the fledgling nationalist group they supported and whose leaders had just been arrested.

They were, they said, going to talk to the prime minister about that, they would walk into the centre of Salisbury if necessary to present their case for the release of their leaders.

At the Stoddart Hall the marchers came to a halt. Across their path stood 500 white-helmeted policemen in full riot gear, truncheons, tear gas and pistols. The police told the crowd that Sir Edgar Whitehead, the premier, had agreed to meet their delegation in the morning. There was a huge cheer. The police stood over them as they bedded down for the night in the middle of the street.

The following morning the word spread quickly through the township about what was happening – the arrests, then the meeting, finally the march, and now a promised meeting with Whitehead.

Half the African labour force in and around Salisbury boycotted work that day, many of them headed off to the Stoddart Hall. By midday the crowd had grown to about 40,000. Among them was Mugabe, home barely a month from Ghana and only passing through at that before going back to Accra. The day was 20 July 1960, the march was called 'The March of the 7000' who started it, and its significance need only be measured by the fact that it finally persuaded Mugabe to commit himself to the nationalist movement.

Mugabe had not returned to Salisbury with the intention of staying very long. He had come back very temporarily to see his mother, still living at Katama, under the generous leave conditions which the Nkrumah government granted expatriate African teachers. It wasn't just a holiday for them: they would also act as informal ambassadors for the achievements of Ghana back in their own countries.

Three young nationalists were to change his mind and make him stay: Michael Mawema, Leopold Takawira and Edgar Tekere. Takawira, a seasoned veteran of the nationalist struggle, having been executive officer of the multi-racial Capricorn Society throughout the 1950s; Mawema, a trade unionist and a nationalist already showing the capability to organise meetings, marches and rallies; and Edgar Tekere, a leader of the Youth Wing of the NDP. All of them had urged Mugabe to remain in Rhodesia and devote his talents, intellect and education to the nationalist struggle. Mugabe had not yet decided, when at dawn on 19 July police raided the homes of Takawira and Mawema.

Now Mugabe was among the crowd outside the Stoddart Hall. It was characteristic of the man that the leadership he showed that day was thrust on him – he did not seek it.

Edgar Whitehead had no intention of seeing the demonstrators, even meeting a delegation from them. Now he was infuriated at the work boycott. When two representatives from the NDP arrived to see him he refused to talk to them and instead went on radio to issue a call-up order for a battalion of the territorial militia. He stopped only to add that all meetings would henceforth be banned in the townships of Salisbury. The crowd heard all this on their radios but they stayed calm, although by now the police had brought in dogs to reinforce their barrier.

During the afternoon, they built a tiny podium and one by one the young men who aspired to lead the teeming thousands outside the Stoddart Hall got up to speak. Mugabe was asked to stand up and address the crowd as well. He was introduced as a distinguished 'Zimbabwean' who had travelled in Africa, who had three university degrees, and who didn't want to have the European lifestyle he might aspire to.

Mugabe was a little nervous to start with. He started by talking about Ghana, what he'd seen happening there, how a new society was being created. His attempts to make the crowd share his vision of Ghana as a model for others was hard work both for Mugabe and his audience.

But when turned to his vision of the nationalist movement in 'Zimbabwe', the crowd warmed to him: first a murmur, then a little, light applause, finally an outburst of hearty clapping.

'The nationalist movement will only succeed if it is based on a blending of all classes of men,' Mugabe said.

'It will be necessary for graduates, lawyers, doctors and others to accept the chosen leadership even if they (the leaders) are not university men.'

The crowd roared their approval, even though they were a little astounded. Here was a man of education and ability, a man who had travelled, a man who could make his way into European society and enjoy all the privileges that entailed: and he was saying he wanted to join battle with them the poor, the uneducated, the peasants. After years of watching Africans seduced by the charms and benefits of European society to which their training gave them access, Mugabe came as something of a novelty.

He stayed on the makeshift podium, from where it was decided that the crowd should remain until they received some positive response from the government.

The following morning they got it. At first the police moved in with their batons. Then the dogs followed. Finally they simply drove their Landrovers into the crowd. Spotter planes buzzed overhead, telling the police exactly where the marchers were dispersing to and so making them easier targets.

The demonstrators retreated to their townships, but the police chased them even there. The marchers set up barricades and road blocks, they stoned police cars and vehicles owned by whites.

By the end of the day, nearly 130 Africans had been arrested, dozens had been wounded, some of them seriously. The townships were littered with rubble from the riot. The following weekend the unrest spread to Bulawayo, and there the police did not hesitate to open fire. Eleven Africans were shot.

The March of the 7000, as it became known, made Mugabe a committed nationalist. It also produced arguably the most repressive legislation from the government to date. The Law and Order (Maintenance) Amendment Act vastly increased the power of the police in handling demonstrators: it also virtually gave the police the right to act with impunity, with not even the scrutiny of the courts to face.

Mugabe wasn't the only one dismayed. For the federal chief justice, Sir Robert Tredgold, it was too much.

'This bill outraged every basic human right,' he said as he resigned. 'It will remove the last vestige of doubt about whether Rhodesia is a police state.'

The demonstration, followed by that bill, was to bring it home all too starkly to Mugabe that the years and the winds of change he'd seen in Ghana were still a long way from Rhodesia.

He had returned home enthusiastic, hoping for signs

of change and expecting at least a greater awareness among Africans in Rhodesia of the prospects of self-rule. Ghana's independence and the years of black rule, which Mugabe had witnessed, were a beacon for the rest of Africa. It signalled not just the possibility of independence, but taught nationalists throughout the continent to think of themselves as one group with a common cause – majority rule – rather than disparate groups of colonial subjects isolated from each other in their attempts to dislodge colonial rulers.

Furthermore, Mugabe had seen in Ghana that the goal of independence and self-rule could be realised. He had come home full of confidence about the prospects for his own country.

His confidence and his enthusiasm was transmitted to the meetings he addressed in the first few weeks after his return. The audience was invariably eager to hear tales from another country and Mugabe quickly became a good story-teller. He would embellish his story of Ghana's development with anecdotes about the people, what they are, always reminding them that they were not so very different from Rhodesians.

The difference, Mugabe would say, is that the Ghanaians rule themselves, they ran their own country. And there was no division between the people of the city and the country, no great divide even between those educated and those not.

Africans like you, he would say as he picked out a man in the audience and asked him what he did, are being appointed to positions in the civil service and industry.

'Yet here the Europeans tell us that we cannot undertake these jobs. Why?' he asked.

He was bitterly upset at the police action outside the Stoddart Hall. He realised that this was to be no Ghana, there were no winds of change coming through his country. As always with Mugabe, his disappointment and dismay was turned into determination. Now he was determined to stay in Rhodesia, now he was determined to join the nationalists wherever it led.

In the eyes of white Rhodesians in 1960, change could only mean change for the worst. Unlike the white traders and administrators of Britain's east and west African colonies, white society in Rhodesia was an integrated, self-sufficient community of farmers, tradesmen, businessmen. Although their cities were not large – Salisbury had a population of 300,000 in those days, of whom 100,000 were white – they were sophisticated by African standards of the day. They had built themselves a lifestyle second to none in Africa.

Moreover, the white population was expanding rapidly: in 1946 there had been 82,000, by 1960 there were 223,000. Predominantly English-speaking, well over half had been born in Britain and in the years after the war friends and relatives from there had moved in regular droves to join the first generations of settlers. It wasn't hard to see why. Their standard of living was high. The average family income of a European in Rhodesia was much higher than in Britain, and the cost of living much lower.

The weather was pleasant and the lifestyle relaxed. Many whites who would have only limited opportunities for success and satisfaction back home, primarily because of their own limited skills and the economic constraints in post-war Britain, found the good life in Rhodesia.

That life, of course, was sustained by the economic, social and political inequality between blacks and whites. And they knew it. So any concessions to the winds of change could only blow apart the society they had stitched so carefully together in cities like Salisbury, Bulawayo and Umtali, towns like Plumtree, Centenary and Inyanga, down on the cattle ranches and on their tobacco farms.

Though many still felt an affinity to Britain, few could

contemplate with equanimity the prospect of returning to the hardships and frustrations they had left behind them. So they dug in. Attitudes, which had rarely been enlightened, hardened. Ideologies which had justified domination of the native population in order to achieve colonisation, were now honed into a new shape and philosophy. It justified their complete domination of Rhodesia, and the comforts of large houses in smart, tidy suburbs, servants, dinner parties, cocktails at the golf club and dinner at a good restaurant. All of which they stood to lose if the blacks got majority rule.

During Mugabe's years in Ghana, events in Rhodesia had not moved forward as there but backwards. The frustrations of the nationalist movement had only increased. Access to power and political decision-making was more restricted than ever. Politics remained an exclusively European affair. Although the voting qualification did not exclude non-Europeans, it was limited to those who met an extraordinary combination of educational and financial requirements. The effect was simple: it gave the vote to virtually all the whites and just a handful of blacks. The number of Africans eligible to vote never exceeded more than a couple of hundred.

The restricted franchise, as it was called, was justified by the Europeans on the grounds that when Africans achieved a level of 'sophistication' and 'civilisation' which education and income implied, they would then be granted a role in governing the State. In this, the effect was divisive for the African community. Those with education and money could make it. They were offered access to European circles. The few who managed to take up the offer argued that entering European society, at whatever level, could only give them the opportunity to convince the whites that all Africans should have the same chance.

Those who took this path during the 1950s and joined the United Rhodesian Party of the then prime minister,

Sir Garfield Todd, or the various mutli-racial groups like the Capricorn Society, the Inter-racial Association or Moral Re-armament, could at the end of the day produce little evidence of tangible results.

Taking tea with nice liberal Europeans was not going to change the lot of the vast majority of Africans in Rhodesia. The short-sightedness of such a strategy by the few educated Africans had been brought home in 1958 when Todd was toppled from the leadership for allegedly liberal views. He was removed for wanting to widen the voting franchise but just as damaging had been his opposition to a bill that sought formally to outlaw sexual relations outside marriage between whites and blacks. On such matters the whites were indeed digging in.

Todd was no radical at that time. He had often been abrasive in dealing with Africans. Mugabe had already had a clash with him during his school-teaching days. As a budgetary measure Todd cut 60 pence from the three pounds a month African teachers earned. Mugabe, on behalf of teachers, challenged him. 'He was an excessively domineering man,' Mugabe said at the time. 'I told him I would box him if necessary.' Having said that, though, Todd did at least offer hope to the Africans. The issues over which he was deposed and replaced by Whitehead killed that – and the belief that any progress could be made through the channels of the Capricorn Society, through 'civilised inter-racial contact' as the whites put it. For the nationalists Todd's overthrow meant they had to look elsewhere for a means to change. Nathan Shamuyarira, now Mugabe's Minister of Information, recalls that the failure of 'inter-racial contact' culminating in Todd's removal spawned serious, hard-line nationalism.

'The most powerful reason was that such contact provoked no response of encouragement from the broad range of government officials or white politicians ... While we sat at the bottom end of town deliberating about equality and human dignity, parliament was still passing restrictive laws like the Public Order Act which gave the government power to use troops in breaking strikes.

'After years of repression, we were looking for quick results. Instead we continued to be humiliated.'

The organisation which was now to point the nationalist movement in a new direction had already been going for two years when Todd was deposed. It was called the City-Youth League.

The Youth League started out avowing confrontation rather than co-operation with the whites.

'Do not hang on the backs of the Europeans like babies,' its leader, James Chikerema, told an inuagural meeting in Harare in 1956. 'Rely now on yourselves!' It was quite unlike the language Africans had hitherto used in public when discussing politics. Unlike its predecessors, the CYL did not request recognition of black claims to equality and a better standard of living by the Europeans. It simply challenged their authority.

That same year it organised a boycott of the buses which carried Africans from the townships to work in Salisbury. Once they had been owned by blacks, now they had been taken over by whites. And they had raised the fares. At the largest public meeting for years, in Chamunika square in Harare, the CYL won widespread support for a boycott. It worked. The government began subsidising fares.

In Rhodesian terms, it was a great victory for the CYL and its policy of challenging rather than asking government.

That success encouraged others. In September 1957 a national movement, the African National Congress (ANC) was launched. It brought together the CYL and the ANC of Bulawayo, which had bean started in the 1930s but had since lapsed into inactivity. Chickerema was not chosen as leader. That went to Joshua Nkomo, a Methodist lay preacher and a one-time leader of railway workers who had a reputation for skilful negotiation. One of the few nationalists with a degree – he had taken an external course in economics and sociology from the University of South Africa – he was seen as a sound, middle-of-the-road figure to challenge the whites on their own level without alienating them, as the more militant Chikerema might have.

Nkomo was careful to stress that the ANC's objective was not to overthrow white authority but to gain, by putting pressure on the whites, some say in how that authority was exercised.

'What we are asking for immediately is therefore direct participation in the territorial legislature and government. And we ask not as suppliants but as people who know their rights cannot indefinitely be withheld from them.'

It wasn't very long before the ANC started winning converts in both the urban and rural areas. In the tribal lands, it challenged the arrogance and contempt with which the native commissioners treated the black population. When they attempted to 'de-stock' land of cattle and crops, ostensibly to prevent deterioration of arable country, the movement questioned their powers to do so. For the first time ever the commissioners, who up till now had acted a law unto themselves, were forced to justify their actions.

Encouraged by the ANC, Africans resisted their attempts to control as they had always done, reported their actions in detail and then challenged their powers in the courts. One party official, George Nyandoro, even took a court action against Prime Minister Whitehead for wrongfully using the Land Husbandry Act against blacks.

Before it got to court, the government moved. A state of emergency was declared. The ANC was banned in 1959, 500 of its members were rounded up, among them Chikerema and Nyandoro. Nkomo was out of the country enlisting support in Cairo and escaped detention.

The pattern was now set. It was to be repeated several times during the next few years. When any nationalist organisation showed the slightest sign of challenging European power, it was quickly banned, its funds and equipment seized and its leaders arrested.

Whitehead's policy was never publicly stated but it was clear. He wanted to crush the nationalist movement while fostering the growth of a loyal black middle class.

His own version was a little different. Initially he justified the state of emergency on the pretext that there had been rioting in the townships. But there hadn't been any serious disorders. In the absence of any insurrection or evidence of a threat to his government, Whitehead explained his action thus:

'It is a very ancient tradition of the British people that governments should defer action against subversive movements until actual rioting or bloodshed has occurred. My government does not subscribe to this tradition. I do not think that it would be an exaggeration to say that the security forces have always been a little in advance of subversive elements in Southern Rhodesia. It had become evident that if these people had been allowed to continue indefinitely in the courses, disorder and probably bloodshed would be the inevitable result. Existing laws were not designed to deal with a subversive movement which had as its ultimate objective the overthrow of all existing authority; and although many prosecutions were instituted it soon became clear that completely new measures were necessary to deal effectively with the menace.'

By the end of 1959, however, Whitehead felt confident enough of his position to release most of the detainees. The ANC was still proscribed, so on New Year's Day 1960 the NDP was formed. Its achievements were to be overshadowed by the parties that succeeded but it remains a watershed in the nationalist politics of Rhodesia.

It did more than just pick up where the ANC had left off. Whereas the ANC under Nkomo had concentrated on agitating against injustice inherent in the Land Husbandry and Land Apportionment laws, the NDP focused on constitutional reform and fundamental political change. No longer did the nationalists demand that Africans be treated fairly and reasonably. The demand now was the abolition of the constitution which automatically produced discriminatory laws.

Takawira, one of its founding fathers, told the first meeting of the party: 'We are no longer asking Europeans to rule us well.

We now want to rule ourselves.'

They were encouraged by events elsewhere. Men like Mugabe were coming home with first-hand accounts of the change in societies like Ghana; Kenya, Nigeria and Somalia were rapidly approaching independence.

Britain showed no sign of being ready to intervene in Rhodesia but the election of John Kennedy in the United States did hold out the promise of a change of direction in American foreign policy. The advent of Kennedy's 'new frontier', the nationalists felt, raised the possibility of American pressure on the colonial powers to force decolonisation quickly.

The NDP, furthermore, had leaders of some potential. There was Ndabiningi Sithole, a minister and teacher who had already produced the best apologia for the nationalist cause, a book entitled *African Nationalism*; Herbert Chitepo, the first black Rhodesian lawyer who had risen from a mission school education to force a change in the Land Apportionment Act that enabled him to have chambers in Salisbury alongside white lawyers; and Mugabe, fresh from Ghana, full of ideas and confidence in the black man's ability to win and use 'one-man one-vote'.

*

Mugabe had made up his mind, or rather had it made up for him, by the rally and ensuing riot outside Stoddart Hall. Within a matter of weeks, in October 1960, the NDP held its first party congress and he was elected publicity secretary.

From this relatively humble position, and within a matter of months, Mugabe proceeded to carry out a major cornerstone of policy which was to be of lasting importance to the nationalist movement in the years ahead.

He'd already been working on it – in those speeches at Kutama and to meetings in the townships – even before he was elected to any position in the party. His aim was to consciously inject emotionalism into the thinking of the nationalists. From his experience in Ghana he recognised that support for the movement would have to rest on something more than just intellectual attraction for men like himself. To win broad-based support among all Africans in Rhodesia, the struggle had to be made part of the people's daily life. The barrier between political activity and all others had to be broken down. The people must be made to recognise politics without the taboo of thinking that it wasn't their domain.

He appealed to their emotions and to their spiritual and cultural values. He encouraged them, through party publicity, to value their heritage. For almost a generation Africans had been taught to scoff at traditional religion, dancing, food, dress, customs, even names. Drawing on his experience from Nkrumah's youth league, Mugabe began organising the NDP Youth Wing with these appeals to search for what he called 'cultural roots'. Nathan Shamuyira has recalled the excitement that Mugabe's leadership of the youth created.

'From the position of publicity secretary, Mugabe proceeded to organise a semi-militant youth wing, which he felt to be a vital arm of the movement. Youth started influencing and controlling some party activities. Thudding drums, ululation by women dressed in national costumes, and ancestral prayers began to feature at meetings more prominently than before. A public meeting became a massive rally of residents of a given township. The Youth Wing, with a small executive taking charge of units of fifty houses in each township, knocked at every door on Saturday evening to remind residents about meetings. Next Sunday morning, thudding drums, and singing groups again reminded the residents, until the meeting started. The usual Sunday pastimes of church, drinking and women were given second place. The last meeting of the NDP, held in Highfield on 3 December 1962, was proof of the emotion that had been evoked. An hour before it was to start, every path was one huge, coiled black snake of wriggling bodies heading for the central Cyril Jennings Hall. At the hall, Youth Leaguers ordered attendants to remove their shoes, ties and jackets, as one of the first signs in rejecting European civilisation. Water served in traditional water-pots replaced Coca-Cola kiosks. By the time the first speaker, a European in bare feet, took the platform, the whole square was a sea of some 15,000 to 20,000 cheering and cheerful black faces. The emotional impact of such gatherings went far beyond claiming to rule the country – it was an ordinary man's participation in creating something new, a new nation.'

Because at the outset Mugabe had intended only to pay a temporary visit to Rhodesia, Sally had returned to Ghana. Now he wrote to her, asking her to join him in Rhodesia and marry him there.

On 21 February 1961 they were married in the simple, white-washed Roman Catholic Church in Harare. It was a formal ceremony. He wore his favourite black suit, Sally a pretty white wedding dress she had brought with her.

Before they were married, they took instructions together. Sally converted to Catholicism. Over the years since they have stopped going to church, but that doesn't mean the church has waned in its influence on them both, which it had clearly had at the time of their marriage. Mugabe recognises even today that the Church first taught him the equality of man, regardless of race, in the eyes of God. The Catholic Church alone was prepared to speak out for that in the early days of the nationalist struggle.

Even on their wedding day, they admitted to each other the uncertainty of their future together. But Sally, then and ever since, harboured no doubts.

'When I went to Zimbabwe,' she says, 'I didn't think I was just going to sit on the fence. I knew when I went that I would be involved.'

She could, however, have scarcely imagined as they exchanged vows what that involvement would cost her and Mugabe. She, like him, was to be imprisoned for her political activities. She, along with him, was to suffer the traumatic loss of their two children in infancy. For years she was to know her husband only through his letters from jail. Nineteen years later, with Mugabe's triumph in the 1980 election, she was to remark simply: 'In nineteen years of marriage, we have had six together.'

By the time of their marriage, the NDP was pursuing a new policy of trying to force Britain to curb the extreme actions of the white government in Salisbury. Britain alone, the leadership felt, could force the whites into conceding the blacks political power.

Now the Foreign Office organised a constitutional conference in Salisbury under the Commonwealth Secretary, Duncan Sandys. The NDP, now led by Nkomo who had returned in November 1960, represented the nationalists. The deal that Nkomo, Sithole and Chitepo accepted was to leave lasting doubts in the minds of subordinates not only about the intentions of the British – but also the commitment and ability of Nkomo. The whites wanted the last vestige of British rule removed the reserve powers which gave Whitehall the right to veto discriminatory legislation. Britain, for its part, wanted to get out of any involvement with Rhodesia constitutionally. The package satisfied them both.

There was to be no further intervention by Britain in Rhodesia's constitutional affairs. In reply, the whites gave the blacks 15 seats in a 65-member parliament. On the basis of this, majority rule was decades away. Nevertheless, even to Duncan Sandys amazement, Nkomo accepted it.

But his subordinates didn't. Takawira, by then directing the NDP's external relations from London, telegrammed his anger. 'We totally reject Southern Rhodesia constitutional agreement as treacherous to future of three million Africans. Agreement diabolical and disastrous. Outside world shocked by NDP docile agreement. We have lost sympathy of friends and supporters. Unless you take firm stand ... future means untold suffering and toil. Pray you denounce uncompromisingly and reject unreserved conference agreement. Demand immediate reversal of present position. Future of three million Africans depends on immediate action.'

Within five days of the conference ending, the NDP executive met and overturned the leadership's agreement to the constitutionally complex franchise arrangements under which the black MPs would have been elected. It was a fierce, at times noisy, debate lasting four hours. Mugabe spoke out bitterly against the bargain struck by Nkomo. It was a sell-out, he said.

At his insistence, the NDP executive had told Nkomo and Sithole during the conference itself that they must get an equal number of seats for blacks as for Europeans. Nothing less. How could Nkomo have accepted such a defeat, he asked?

Nkomo was furious. He left the meeting muttering threats of action against Takawira, and Mugabe.

In March, the NDP held a national congress. Young

representatives from all over Rhodesia endorsed the executive's rejection of the franchise but agreed to participate in a referendum to be held on the constitutional package. For that, though, they wanted concessions from Prime Minister Whitehead – the release of all ANC detainees and the lifting of the ban on rural meetings. Whitehead refused. A further congress voted at once to boycott the referendum.

Mugabe and his colleagues in the Youth Wing designed ingenious ways of getting round the law to campaign for a boycott. The ban on rural meetings could prevent them from getting their message over to the vast majority of Africans out in the country. Now NDP supporters, under Mugabe's instructions, boarded buses carrying blacks from work to home and held impromptu meetings on board. Out in the tribal areas, they would call people from the villages out into the open bush. By the time the police arrived from the nearest town the meeting was either over – or if it wasn't the NDP turned it into a perfectly legal party.

By now Mugabe was not just attracting the attention of Nkomo and other NDP leaders, he was also coming under the watchful eye of the police special branch.

In April 1961, the public at large heard of him for the first time. The Salisbury newspapers reported a fierce row between 'a Robert Mugabe' and the police at Salisbury airport. The police had accused an NDP supporter of carrying a weapon on the airport grounds.

'We are taking over this country and we will not put up with this nonsense,' Mugabe told the police.

It was a first hint of what was to come.

In July that year Nkomo returned from a trip to London with bad news. He had a conversation with a junior British minister, the Duke of Devonshire. The duke had told him that, because of the large amount of British investment in Rhodesia, Britain would not hand over power to the Africans. It feared political instability too much.

The NDP's reaction was immediate. No one mentioned the word 'war', but the executive agreed on a strategy to make British investors and companies realise that their holdings in the country would be endangered more by the political unrest that would inevitably grow with white minority rule than by an uncertainty created by Africans coming to power.

It was left to Mugabe to announce the new NDP policy of 'positive action'.

'Europeans,' he said, 'must realise that unless the legitimate demands of African nationalism are recognised, then racial conflict is inevitable.'

In conjunction with this, publicity secretary Mugabe announced a campaign of self-denial which would indicate, he said, the willingness of the Africans to make sacrifices to achieve their goal.

Fasts were organised and there was a boycott of the beer halls in the townships. At NDP meetings shoes were removed – a symbol, it was said, of rejection of the white man's custom.

On 3 December 1961, Mugabe told the 20,000 supporters at a rally in Salisbury: 'Today you have removed your shoes. Tomorrow you may be called upon to destroy them altogether, or to perform other acts of self-denial.

'If European industries are used to buy guns which are aimed against us, we must withdraw our labour and our custom and destroy those industries.'

Language like that was enough for the government. Within six days of the meeting the NDP was banned, its funds and vehicles were seized, its leaders prohibited from addressing any public meetings for four months.

As his language had showed, however, Mugabe and the NDP were prepared for it this time. In contrast to the confusion which followed the banning of the ANC in 1959, the nationalists neatly circumvented the law to carry on.

Within 10 days of the ban on the NDP, it was replaced by the Zimbabwe African Peoples Union (Zapu). The executive remained largely the same. It even included Chikerema and Nyandoro, who had remained in detention since the crackdown on the ANC in 1959.

At first, the government replied with an increase in the powers they already had under the draconian Unlawful Organisations and Law and Order (Maintenance) Acts. Now someone could be imprisoned for up to 10 years for demanding that another join a political party.

But that wasn't enough to stop Zapu building support just as the NDP had done before it. Within nine months, in September 1962, Zapu was banned and its leaders put under restriction orders for three months.

Mugabe was sent to a tribal reserve about 50 miles from Salisbury. His home was a mud hut with a tin roof. An English professor, Claire Palley, saw Mugabe during the restriction period.

'I was enormously impressed by him,' she says. 'The quality most apparent was his intellectual rigour. He had this ability to listen to argument, then dissect it, take it to bits.

'His politics at this time? He struck me as not so much a doctrinaire Marxist but an old-fashioned African nationalist. Even then I would have put him among the top four or five black leaders in Rhodesia.'

Later Mrs Palley saw him holding a meeting with party supporters. Already, she says, he had developed the 'collectivist' style which was to be a hallmark of his leadership in years to come.

'Everything was thrashed out by everybody. Mugabe himself was a very good chairman ... he was very good at keeping order and very fair with all of them, giving them a hearing.'

But Mugabe at this stage lacked the confidence to

43

assume the leadership the party needed so desperately in the face of the government crack-down. And now the actions of Joshua Nkomo, his initial indecisiveness and then his ill-conceived strategy of leaving Rhodesia, were to undermine seriously whatever attempts the nationalists made to regain ground.

The ban on Zapu and the restrictions on its leaders found Nkomo out of the country. This had been the case when the ANC leaders were detained in 1959 and it was to be a characteristic of Nkomo's political leadership that his emphasis on international support rather than consolidation of his domestic political base meant that his international reputation as a leader of the nationalist struggle was considerably greater than his domestic following. His international activities and his frequent absence from Rhodesia meant that he avoided detention several times when most of the other senior nationalist leaders were incarcerated in Rhodesia.

On the day of the ban and the detentions, Nkomo was in Lusaka conferring with President Kenneth Kaunda, on the final leg of an international trip. He was due back in Salisbury within a day or so. Nathan Shamuyarira recalls: 'It was expected that Nkomo would return home at once to give leadership to his followers. Instead, after a few days hesitation, he decided to motor to Dar-es-Salaam despite being advised against this by the nationalist leaders in Zambia.'

Only after the repeated urgings of other nationalists and after another member of the Zapu executive, Ndabaningi Sithole, had flown from a conference which he was attending in Athens to talk to him, was Nkomo persuaded that he should provide the moral leadership required by returning home and facing restriction with the others. Nkomo did. But his inability to make a decision and stick to it cost both him and his party dearly.

Before the restriction period was finished he summoned the Zapu executive to the Somukwe reserve near Plumtree, where he was detained. He argued that they should all leave Rhodesia and establish a government in exile. Everyone, including Mugabe who had exposed himself to considerable danger by leaving his own restriction area, rejected the proposal.

In December, just as the Zapu leaders were being allowed free, Whitehead's government was defeated in a general election by the newly formed Rhodesia Front led by Winston Field, Clifford Dupont and Ian Smith. For them, even Whitehead's minor concessions like integration in schools, hospitals and residential areas, were too much. Field and his first government felt even less constrained than their predecessors by the niceties of the British legal process when it came to handling the nationalist 'fanatics', as they called them. At once there were amendments to the Law and Order (Maintenance) Act. Now there was a mandatory death sentence for saboteurs. Mugabe was allowed to go as these amendments were being passed. He travelled to Zambia, where he addressed a public meeting.

The reforms to the Act were, he said, 'Legislation for murder.' He warned of what the Field government would do.

'This fascist settler cowboy government is preparing to unilaterally declare Rhodesia independent from Britain for the settlers to subject millions of Africans to slavery.'

When he returned to Rhodesia, three months later, he was arrested and charged with a series of offences, including 'making a subversive statement within the hearing of others.' The trial date was set and he was released on bail.

He wasn't the only one in the middle of a legal battle. By now Sally was as well. In one of those precious ironies of Rhodesian history, the government which was to declare UDI charged her with 'making subversive statements likely to bring the Queen into hatred and contempt' with a speech to a party meeting in which she bitterly

45

attacked Britain for abandoning the blacks in Rhodesia and said: 'The Queen can go to hell.'

She had already been sentenced to two years imprisonment for the offence (15 months of it suspended subject to her refraining from political activity). Now she was released on bail pending an appeal.

Nkomo had also been arrested and charged for holding a meeting in the town of Rusape, east of Salisbury. He too waited on an appeal.

Again Nkomo changed his mind and tried to go against the wishes of his executive. This time he succeeded. In a meeting lasting five days, he persuaded them to leave the country and set up headquarters in Dar-es-Salaam. Mugabe led the opposition along with Takawira and Sithole, insisting that whatever the punishment of staying they must show to the people they would stick it out rather than allow them to believe they were unwilling to make the sacrifices they had urged on others.

Nkomo held the trump card. He had just returned from a trip overseas. It was, he said, the view of the African leaders and President Nyererere of Tanganyika in particular that they should leave Rhodesia and fight the Field government from exile than stay and be stranded through the detention that was inevitable.

Mugabe's final impassioned plea failed. His disappointment at Nkomo's stance was eased only by the belief that if their allies in Zambia and Tanganyika wanted them to leave, they must. He already knew war was inevitable – and he knew that Nyerere and Kaunda could decide the outcome of that war with the help they might give.

But for the Mugabes the trip was particularly dangerous. Not only were both he and Sally on bail and liable for arrest if they were caught attempting to leave. Now Sally was well into a difficult pregnancy. They had already lost their first child at birth a year before and the constant moves and threat of detention were making this second pregnancy equally problematic for Sally.

They decided, by themselves, to go: they were pinning their hopes on the support and encouragement Nyerere had apparently promised. They were to be shocked on arrival in Dar-es-Salaam. Nyerere told them all he was surprised, indeed amazed, at their decision to leave Rhodesia. It was very ill-advised.

Not only was Zapu's presence in Dar-es-Salaam not welcomed. The funds which Nkomo had told the executive would be available to them failed to materialise. They didn't even have enough money to house the executive and their families, let alone the cash to buy and send equipment back to Rhodesia. Mugabe was angry and depressed. Cut off from the political movement which he felt he should be back home organising, his frustration and sense of betrayal by Nkomo festered for weeks. He made no secret of his belief that Nkomo had to go.

In May, when a six-man Zapu team went to Addis Ababa to lobby support from the Organisation of African Unity (OAU), Mugabe challenged Nkomo. He had more than just reservations about Nkomo's tactics. He knew they were wrong, that Nkomo was set on a course to disaster. Sithole and Takawira supported him. But he still lacked the power and the position to get rid of Nkomo. The leadership question remained an unsolved doubt.

The views of the OAU certainly weren't that. Their message was the same as that of Nyerere and Kaunda: go home and organise, show that you have the support to fight the struggle and then we will assist you.

Even Nkomo couldn't resist the pressure now. When they returned to Dar-es-Salaam there was a letter from Kaunda telling him that he must return to Rhodesia immediately. Nyerere gave him the same order personally at State House. Nkomo cancelled a trip to Yugoslavia and went back. It wasn't total sacrifice, he was hoping he could ward off the plans of the 'rebels' like Mugabe and Sithole to remove him. There he found evidence of a plot – letters which Eddison Zvobgo, a bright young

47

lawyer, had brought from the 'rebels' in Dar-es-Salaam, saying the executive no longer supported Nkomo and telling the party in Salisbury to prepare for a change in leadership.

Letters in his hand, Nkomo called a press conference and announced that four members of the executive were suspended immediately: party chairman Washington Malianga, Sithole, Takawira, and Mugabe.

In Dar-es-Salaam the following day the split was made complete. The seven members of the executive there voted, four to three, to replace Nkomo with Sithole. It was a breach that was never to be properly healed in the 18 years of struggle ahead.

The agony of the decision now facing Mugabe was to haunt him for years. The politician in him told him to go back to Salisbury, even though it meant arrest and detention. The private man said stay and wait for their child to be born. Mugabe knew Nkomo would be turning his own argument – of making the sacrifice and going home – against him. But he stayed and in August, Sally gave birth to a son. They named the child Nhamodzenyika, Shona for 'suffering country'. 'The baby', said Mugabe years later, was 'a sign of hope in the centre of a storm.'

The next four months were the only ones Mugabe would have with his child. For a few precious weeks, he was a father rather than a politician. His enormous affection for children and the delight he takes in being with them is apparent to this day. It was all the more noticeable during the short time he had with Nhamodzenyika.

He worked painstakingly at winning friends for the movement in Dar-es-Salaam, there were endless meetings with ambassadors and OAU officials who would be needed in the future. But his mind was more on Sally and the baby.

Nkomo now moved quickly to consolidate his position and quell the rebellion before it gathered any momentum.

He called a conference of the party for 10 August.

When the rebels heard they countered immediately. Two days before it, a meeting was called at the home of Zapu militant Enos Nkala in Highfields. Sithole was presented as the leader of the new breakaway party, the Zimbabwe African National Union (Zanu).

While Nkomo was to spell out a policy of isolating the government politically and economically, through pressure on Britain from the international community, Zanu was to dedicate itself from the start to the armed struggle. Little did any of them, Mugabe included, realise just how long it would take them to make the armed struggle a reality.

By December, with the baby just three months old, the Mugabes made up their minds. They both faced certain imprisonment if they went back and, much as Sally detested the idea of separation, she did not resist when Mugabe insisted that she could not go with him. She would take the child to Ghana, to her parents; he would go home to a Rhodesian jail.

The same month he returned to Salisbury. With him was Herbert Chitepo, who was to act as his lawyer. He was arrested on arrival and remanded in custody until his trial. It lasted from January until March 1964.

Mugabe's speeches from the dock stand as a testimony to his dedication to the struggle throughout the long years of imprisonment that followed.

He refused to retract any of the subversive statements he was accused of. He repeated his warning that the government would declare UDI, he denounced once more the 'hanging' clauses in the Law and Order Act. And he insisted, as he was sentenced to 21 months, that he had not fled Rhodesia to avoid the charges.

'It was necessary in the interests of the nation that I took speedy action and left,' he told the court. 'We all had to sacrifice our personal interests to the interests of the nation and get to Dar-es-Salaam where a certain move was being contemplated (by Zapu).

'I questioned the advisability of the move. I thought it was unwise ... but I had to forget my personal interests. As I had foreseen it the move did not materialise and I came back home. It was my own decision.'

Chapter 3 — Prison

For 11 years, beginning with his arrest on his return to Salisbury from Dar-es-Salaam in December 1963 and ending in December 1974 with the 'detente' talks, Mugabe was to spend almost his every moment behind the bars of Rhodesia's jails and detention centres.

It was not just frighteningly lonely, but in the beginning nomadic as well. Mugabe was moved time and again from prison to prison as the government tried to prevent the formation of nationalist 'blocks' in any one of their jails. He started off in Salisbury prison, was moved to Wha Wha detention centre near the midlands town of Gwelo, then transferred to Sikombela jail at Que Que. Only in 1966, when he was taken to Salisbury, to the remand section of the prison, was he to know anything like stability. He remained there for eight years.

Mugabe himself says it is impossible for anyone who has never experienced it to understand the anguish of being moved so frequently. 'It relieved the tedium but made us all so much more uncertain and frightened ... we were at the mercy of people we could never trust and from whom we had little or no information as to what was in store for us.'

What awaited them at the end of the long ride in an enclosed prison van were the most severe living conditions. At Wha Wha, Mugabe was kept along with other political detainees in a dark, squalid cell. A bucket in the corner served as a toilet for half a dozen men. By day the cell was unbearably hot, by night often extremely cold. There were not enough beds to go round and they had to take turns in sleeping on the floor. Sickness followed inevitably. Some did not survive, locked up as they were at Wha Wha for 23 hours a day.

51

In the face of this, Mugabe strove desperately to build up discipline and morale not only in himself but also in the men who would one day join him in freedom and the revolution. From the moment of his arrest, he started fighting battles with the authorities – a way of keeping his mind alive under the crucifying tedium of prison life, as well as establishing his leadership potential with his fellow inmates.

He wanted political status at his trial in early 1964 on subversion charges. And he wanted the same for all the detainees. At first he was held in Salisbury along with common criminals, he was not allowed to study and his access to reading material was limited. Through constant complaints and bickering, he obtained the status he wanted and by the time he was moved the government was beginning to concede that men like Mugabe could be kept apart from the criminals, in 'political wings' of their jails.

Nevertheless, the government had effectively crushed the nationalist movements by the simple tactic of arresting their leaders. Within three months of Mugabe's arrest, nearly 150 Zapu and Zanu leaders were detained. Two months later Nkomo was sent to a detention centre at Gonakudzingwa, in south-east Rhodesia. Finally, in June 1964 Mugabe was joined in prison by Sithole, facing the same subversion charges.

In August the government banned both Zanu and Zapu and arrested the few militants still at large.

From them and Sithole Mugabe learned of the disarray and the wrangling that was tearing the nationalist movement apart. There was now, they said, open warfare between Zanu and Zapu. The anger which the nationalists had previously channelled against the white institutions was now turned back on the African community.

Groups of supporters of both parties fought frequently, and violently. The homes of those who had openly allied themselves with one side or the other were burned: some

52

who barricaded themselves inside died in the blazes. Mob rule had taken over in the African townships of Salisbury and some of the tribal trust lands where the parties had been winning support.

The government was prepared to stand back and let it happen. The inter-party warfare, so long as it was confined to the African communities, reinforced their argument that the Africans were simply not capable or worthy of having any role in running the country.

Mugabe was dismayed, indeed fearful of a total collapse in the movement. But at Sikombela detention centre he saw the opportunity to reverse the course to disaster.

Sikombela had been specially chosen for the growing number of detainees. At first it was barbed wire enclosure right off the dusty, humid and inhospitable Que Que bushland north of Gwelo. The government built homes for the guards. It left the prisoners to make their own mud huts.

They had already built most of them when they heard Mugabe was on his way from Wha Wha. In his honour the Zanu detainees built him a home of his own – a thatched 'daga' hut with a door made painstakingly from reeds. They put him next to his mentor, Leopold Takawira.

A meeting of the Zanu executive was called as Mugabe arrived. He took the floor to deliver the first of many speeches in detention. He offered them only hard work and the faith that they would succeed.

They should not expect quick release, rather years in places like Sikombela. They should not expect the masses to rise in their support, it would take years for them to build an army that could threaten the government.

They must have faith, however, in their ability to win majority rule, and independence. In the meantime, therefore, they had to use their time in prison to prepare for liberation. 'These months, these years, however long it takes, must not be wasted,' he said.

53

Classes in all levels of education would be run by the detainees, he said. Those who already had some education would teach those with little or none, using books and materials which the government was allowing through from aid organisations like Christian Aid and Christian Care. These classes would be in the morning: in the afternoon the 'teachers' would do their own studying. Within a day, meetings of the detainees elected teachers for all levels, ranging from the most junior primary school grade to the Rhodesian certificate level. A day after that school opened. Mugabe was headmaster, with overall responsibility for supervising classes.

He himself had already started studying for a law degree through a correspondence course from the University of London. His own timetable was as busy as it had ever been in his days as a schoolteacher. He was studying himself and spending hours teaching, encouraging and correcting others.

One of his fellow detainees there, who taught in the morning and then received tuition from Mugabe in the afternoon for an English GCE 'O level' examination, recalled years later: 'It was the first time that I witnessed a person turning the nights into days. Mugabe would read and type throughout the night.

Then at sunrise he would simply wash and join the others in the daily routine of washing plates and getting ready for morning classes.

'Every morning there was a hush in and around the whole camp. Occasional visitors were even advised to come in the afternoons in order to leave time for teaching and studying.'

The routine, the orderliness and self-discipline Mugabe preached at Sikombela has remained his own hallmark. To this day he maintains the practice, which he started during detention, of rising at 5 a.m. and doing what he calls 'my yoga': a combination of calisthenics and meditation. His censorious attitude towards smokers, which is more than just the irritation of a non-smoker to tobacco smell, also goes back to Sikombela. He says he saw too many men involved in needless fights over a cigarette. Today, his personal staff and those regularly in his company are almost all non-smokers. One of his body-guards once joked that he'd got his job with Mugabe because he was a non-smoker.

The education, the discipline, the routine gave a purpose to life in centres like Sikombela. It did not, however, ease the harsh living conditions. The poor quality and the lack of variety of food took a toll of everyone's health. The prisoners cooked their own food from rations which were brought to the detention centre by the police, usually on Fridays. If they were lucky, they got a small amount of meat which they would dry in the sun so they could eke it out without it rotting. If they weren't, it was an endless diet of beans and maize-meal which they would cook into traditional sadza porridge. It is another legacy of prison life that even today Mugabe still eats sadza.

On 11 November 1965 Ian Smith announced Rhodesia's Unilateral Declaration of Independence from Britain. The first Mugabe knew of it was when security was strengthened at Sikombela and he asked the new warders why. The Smith regime feared that UDI would spark off an increase in sabotage and guerrilla activity. An attempt to free the detainees at Sikombela was suspected by the authorities. The fact was that Zanu and Zapu were too disorganised to mount any serious challenge to Smith or UDI.

From Sikombela the Zanu executive set up clandestine communications to the party militants still at large in Rhodesia and abroad. Some of the African warders, even though they worked for one of the more repressive arms of the Smith regime, were nevertheless sympathetic to the cause. They smuggled out letters to the activists. One reached Chitepo, by now in Lusaka organising the very small army of guerrillas. In it Chitepo was told by the executive that he now had the power to organise the external wing of the party. It was to be called the war council – the Dare re chimurenga – which was to assume overall responsibility for Zanu's affairs while the leadership remained in detention. Its purpose was simple: to wage war. In April 1966 a group of 14 Zanu guerrillas infiltrated Rhodesia from Zambia. Their attempts to destroy electrical power pylons at Sinoia failed. They were ill-equipped and poorly trained and badly led. But in a raid on a white farm near Hartley, just 50 miles from Salisbury, they killed farmer Hendrik Viljoen and his wife. Within days they had all been killed by the security forces. Zanu glorified the failure by calling it 'the battle of Sinoia'. That it most certainly was not. But it was the symbolic starting-point of the guerrilla war for independence. The penetration of the guerrillas so far into Rhodesia and so close to Salisbury, backed up by the willingness of the men to turn their guns on a European, boosted the nationalists immeasurably. It also left a dent, however small, in European self-confidence. It was a measure of the panic which the Sinoia incident produced among the Europeans that shortly afterwards the government transferred the Zanu executive and 30 other Zanu detainees to the remand section of Salisbury central prison.

Mugabe and his fellow prisoners might have expected conditions to improve in Salisbury. Instead 40 of them were held in four communal cells designed to take half that number. Again there were not enough mattresses and for months many of them slept on cold, concrete floors.

And again Mugabe insisted on discipline and education as the only answer to the tedium and harshness of prison life. He pushed ahead at a furious speed with his own study. It was no idle or indulgent acquisition of university qualifications. When asked by friends why he was studying so hard, he would say: 'I do it for myself and

Zimbabwe because I know that one day we both will need these degrees.'

For students in his situation a degree in law would normally have taken three to four years. After 18 months, Mugabe was urging London University to let him sit the examination, so he could move on to something else.

He never actually met his tutors, but they got a very clear idea of the man from their long-distance tutorials via the post.

'I got the very definite impression that he was occupying his intellect for the tasks ahead,' recalls one of his tutors who called Mugabe his 'Japanese student' because of his appetite for books. 'He devoured books at such an amazing rate. He knew exactly what he wanted to do, so much so that it became a struggle to impress on him that for the purpose of this exercise I – not he – was the boss. For me it was like trying to ride a very strong-willed horse. He reminded me of Nehru – the same single-mindedness.'

Apart from education, the other main 'outlet' in prison was religion. Many of the detainees had been raised in Christian communities and educated in mission schools. The Church has remained a formidable influence on many Zanu leaders to this day, even those who are no longer church-goers.

It was during his first year in Salisbury prison, in late 1966, that Mugabe suffered the greatest personal tragedy of his life. Visits were few and far between. Occasionally Jack Grant and his wife Ida from Christian Care would be allowed to see him and hand over books and paper. But as time went on, they were more and more restricted. At first visitors like the Grants would mingle with the detainees in the court-yard. But by the late 1960s they, and even those teaching the prisoners, were allowed only to talk to them by telephone while the visitor and the detainee stood either side of a plate glass window. All conversations were thus monitored.

One morning he was summoned to an interview room. There he found Inspector Tony Bradshaw of the Rhodesian police special branch, a prison guard and his sister Sabina. Tears were running down her cheeks.

She told him that his son Nhamodzenyika had died from encephalytis – cerebral malaria – at the home of Sally's parents in Ghana. Sally's sister Esther, a doctor herself, saw the baby in hospital. 'If from the very beginning, the baby had been strong, he might have survived. But the difficult conditions under which he was conceived and raised made him particularly susceptible to any infection.'

Mugabe does not cry easily. But he sobbed openly when he heard the news and could not be consoled for days afterwards. He implored the governor to allow him temporary release from detention, to go to Ghana to bury his son and be with Sally, however briefly. He was hoping against hope that they would grant him permission.

Mugabe had had numerous confrontations with Bradshaw in the past and had no reason to believe that he had any particular sympathy for him. Yet Bradshaw also petitioned the government to allow him three months parole on condition that he guaranteed a return to detention.

Bradshaw believed that Mugabe could be trusted to abide by the conditions, and reasoned that if permission was granted it might give the government some influence with Mugabe. Nothing came of either plea. The government refused to consider the idea.

Almost every leading figure in Zanu can point to some personal tragedy during the years of detention and war. Over the years many of them have recalled them in explaining the resentment and bitterness felt towards the whites. The death of his son was Mugabe's, but it provoked profound sorrow rather than anger in him. Anger was to follow four years later when Takawira died because of the wilful neglect of the prison authorities. He had undiagnosed diabetes, a condition which even the most cursory medical examination would have detected. In the six months prior to his death Takawira's weight fell from 195 to 145 pounds, but the prison doctor insisted it was a psychological conditions.

Mugabe's anguish and dismay and the death of the boy and the ensuing row over whether he should be paroled was rarely shown – certainly not to the prison authorities, and only occasionally to his fellow prisoners. He threw himself into his study, burying his sadness in his determination to survive. Now Sally, who left Ghana after the death of the child, was to help him.

Deprived of her son and of the companionship of her husband, Sally resolved that she too would prepare herself for the time when Rhodesia was free and independent and would be in need of skilled Africans. Before their move to Tanganyika in 1963, and, ironically on the evening of her own release from prison, Sally and Robert had dined in Salisbury with Denis Grennan of the Ariel Foundation. The evening was memorable. The staff stood to attention as they arrived and anyone else had little chance of getting served as all eyes were rivetted on the Mugabe party.

It had been decided that in the event of Robert being imprisoned the Ariel Foundation would provide a scholarship for Sally in London. A number of courses were available, and when the time came she chose to take a degree at Queen Elizabeth College at London University in Home Economics, concentrating on diet and nutrition: areas of neglect in Rhodesia's colonial society. She remained in London until 1975, working at the Runnymede Trust after she had finished her degree.

It was a period of intense activity into which Sally, like Mugabe, threw herself with characteristic vigour. She attended many receptions where she met British members of parliament, who she lobbied fervently, at times following them back to the House of Commons to continue her case for Mugabe's release and the future of her adopted country. Rather than throwing her lot in with the miliantly left wing and anti-apartheid groups she concentrated on those in power, a strategy which later proved invaluable as the wheels of bureacratic red tape turned against her.

As a Ghanaian, and no longer a student, she had no adequate visa to remain in Britain. Had she been Rhodesian the situation would have been different. The fact that she was Robert Mugabe's wife was never questioned, it is unlikely that anyone dealing in alien's visas had even heard of him. It was a simple question of bureacracy and precedent. There was no precedent for her to remain, therefore she should go. She had made many friends at Westminster who collectively wrote to the Home Secretary, pointing out the consequences of deporting the wife of a political prisoner. Eventually she was 'without precedent' allowed to stay.

Many of her evenings were spent in London's libraries summarising, and sometimes copying out in full, books for Mugabe's studies in jail. In the early 1970s the Rhodesian prison authorities had imposed a number of restrictions on study material for the detainees, limiting the number of books they received and forcing them to surrender the books to the prison authorities when courses were complete, thus preventing them being passed on to other detainees embarking on similar courses. The only means around such restrictions was for Sally to make copies of the references Mugabe required and send these copies to him as letters. Elizabeth Walston, wife of a Labour peer in the House of Lords, became a close friend of Sally's during those days in London.

She remembers Sally as 'a quiet power in her own right'.

'The way she wrote out Robert's law books by hand was quite extraordinary, she used to spend hours writing them out line by line. All the time she was so terribly concerned about Robert in detention. I remember she worried about him having blankets. We organised getting blankets out to him. But he never got them.'

Even with the burden which the 11 years of enforced separation from Mugabe imposed on her, and the pressures she herself had had to bear, she showed a fierce determination to help others and a talent for organisation. During her years in London she helped establish a multi-racial college for women; mainly women who had come to London with their husbands from Third World countries and who, because of language and cultural barriers, would otherwise have been isolated in London's alien environment. She had herself suffered from racism in England, particularly from those who considered her husband a 'terrorist' whose imprisonment was justly deserved. The college was very successful and was eventually taken over and run by the Inner London Education Authority

The years 1967 and 1968 were a low point in nationalist activity in Zimbabwe. The Sinoia 'battle' had heartened the nationalists with the knowledge that their guerrillas were able and prepared to attack Europeans. But for two years afterwards, the nationalist cause failed to make any headway. More guerrilla groups were infiltrated into Zimbabwe from Zambia and Tanzania but the results were disappointing.

Many of the fighters were inadequately armed and trained. Since UDI the Smith regime had strengthened the security forces and the straight-forward military problems which the guerrillas faced had increased. It became increasingly difficult to infiltrate undetected and make strikes against targets, the destruction of which it was hoped would serve as symbolic rallying points to the nationalist cause. Since the banning of Zapu and Zanu in 1964 and the detention en masse of party leaders the covert civil politics of the nationalists had lapsed into inactivity. Activists had been detained, increased security meant that people were reluctant to be identified in any way with the nationalist cause and many of those who had done so before fled as refugees to Zambia and Tanzania. In the villages people became more docile and compliant, refusing to be involved in any form of activity which would bring them to the attention of the authorities. In the townships people were too frightened about job security – or rather the lack of it – to risk their livelihood by engaging in political activity.

The Smith regime introduced stiff penalties for failing to report the presence of guerrillas. Retribution was taken against whole villages when guerrillas were detected in an area: the government would take their cattle or drive them off their land. It was a vicious circle for the nationalists: because the level of guerrilla activity was so low they were unable to offer protection against the punishment meted out to the villages for assisting them, so the villages were unwilling to assist the guerrillas and not infrequently betrayed them to the security forces.

Against this background of a weakened nationalist movement, the Wilson Labour Government, which had come to power in Britain 12 montsh before UDI, resumed its talks with the Smith regime.

In the months before UDI Wilson had held talks with Smith in a desperate effort to avoid the impending UDI and in October 1965, a month before Smith made the breach with Britain, Wilson had flown to Salisbury for talks. In Salisbury he had spoken to the representatives of virtually all political positions in Zimbabwe. He had even managed to force Smith to temporarily release Nkomo and Sithole from detention to enable him to talk with them. But Wilson's strategy had been to prevent UDI by attempting to reach some agreement with the Smith regime based on acceptance of the 1961 constitution, plus additional safeguards which would guarantee that there would be no retrogressive amendment to the constitution affecting the position of Africans in Zimbabwe and a vague promise that there would be an improvement in the political status of Africans in Zimbabwe. The nationalists had, however, rejected the 1961 constitution (after the intitial indecisiveness of Nkomo at the 1960 constitutional conference in Salisbury) before it was introduced and Nkomo and Sithole made it clear to Wilson that they were not going to retreat from that stand now, in 1965.

Wilson remained eager to extract Britain from Rhodesia, particularly as his government's failure to take any action against the illegal UDI had made Britain a target for increasing criticism within the United Nations and the Commonwealth.

In 1966 Smith and Wilson held talks on board the cruiser HMS *Tiger* moored at Gibraltar. These collapsed and in October 1968 fresh talks were held on board HMS *Fearless*, again moored at Gibraltar. On both occasions the talks centred on the 1961 constitution and Wilson made it clear that Britain would be prepared to grant independence on the basis of the 1961 constitution, plus some additional safeguards for Africans in Zimbabwe.

The *Fearless* talks concluded with the proposals still on the table and an agreement between Smith and Wilson to discuss the proposals with their own parties and other interested groups.

On 7 November George Thomson, British Minister for State without Portfolio, who had special responsibility for Rhodesia, and Maurice Foley, Foreign and Commonwealth Minister, flew into Sarum Airforce base in Salisbury. There they had a 90-minute talk with Mugabe, Takawira and Sithole. In order to prevent the conversation being bugged by the Zimbabwe authorities they walked to the centre of the base and there, under a tree, Foley and Thomson told the Zanu representatives what had emerged from the *Fearless* talks – precious little.

The two ministers said that although Wilson had not been able to achieve all that might have been desired at the conference 'half a loaf is better than no loaf at all'. In view of Wilson's willingness to conduct talks on the basis of the 1961 constitution, this was a somewhat liberal rendering of its results.

The Zanu representatives were furious that Wilson had been prepared to conduct discussions about the 1961 constitution. To do so undermined the nationalists' position and any achievements which had been made towards majority rule over the previous eight years. And anyway, the African people had already rejected the 1961 constitution. Thomson countered that at least acceptance of the agreement would guarantee the nationalists freedom of political activity, which they did not presently have.

In reply to Mugabe's challenge that Britain had the means to put down what amounted to an illegal seizure of power, Thomson said that Britain had ruled out the use of force. 'It would be an invasion,' he claimed. It would have to be done from Zambia as Britain had no nearby base. 'There would be lots of bloodshed. It is easy to start a war. But a war is like a bushfire which once it starts flares up and spreads. You don't know where it will end.'

To this Mugabe said: 'Surely you have used force elsewhere, in identical situations? We choose to believe, therefore, that the reason you won't use force is because of your kith and kin.' Takawira added: 'We cannot believe that you cannot use force. What does "cannot do it" really mean? Are your soldiers fewer than those of Mr Smith? Is your airforce smaller? What is your fear – a bloodbath?'

'That's right,' replied Foley, 'it is a moral issue.'

Takawira again: 'You are going away, leaving Africans in the hands of these people here. Which to you is the greater moral issue? To leave us at the mercy of these people here and in danger, or to use force, shed some blood but put things right? Remember these Europeans could do anything with the African people here – they could use their military force, detain them all. Nor can we explain to them that the British Government in reality cannot use force. They will not believe us. If Swaziland had been invaded before it became independent would the British have sat back?'

'In Swaziland we had an army and a police force,' replied Thomson. 'We would have certainly put down any rebellion. We had an army there.'

Mugabe, in an effort to clarify Britain's refusal to act, then asked: 'Are the prospects as you see them that South Africa would fight here if you used force?'

'I have no doubt that they would fight. I have had several meetings with South African officials and I am left in no doubt that South Africa would fight,' Thomson replied.

On this dismal note the meeting ended. Thomson and Foley flew back to Britain and the Zanu detainees were driven back to Salisbury gaol.

The proposals went into limbo. The nationalists made it clear that they would never consider themselves bound by any agreement based on the 1961 constitution and the Smith regime baulked at the proposal to restore appeals to the Privy Council.

In June 1970 the Conservative Party, under Sir Alec Douglas-Home, was returned to government and negotiations with the Smith regime were resumed yet again. This time agreement was reached not on the basis of the 1961 constitution but for independence based on the even more restrictive franchise of a new republican constitution which Smith had introduced in 1969.

Agreement was reached between the two governments, subject to some sign that the settlement was acceptable to the 'people of Rhodesia as a whole'. A referendum of African opinion was ruled out and instead the British government sent a commission, chaired by Lord Pearce to investigate the attitude of Zimbabweans to the settlement. To the surprise of the Tory Government the commission reported that 'the people of Rhodesia as a whole do not regard the proposals as a basis for independence'. And that plan, too, was confined to the scrap-heap of history.

Well before the *Fearless* talks the Zanu detainees, led by Mugabe, were harbouring serious doubts about the leadership of Sithole. He had failed to adjust to imprisonment. He was not only permanently irritable, they said, his behaviour was also irrational – to the point where other members of the executive committee conspired to take decisions without him. They then presented them to him as fait accompli.

Shortly after the *Fearless* talks Sithole suggested to Maurice Nyagumbo, an executive member, an assassanation attempt on Ian Smith and two other Rhodesia Front ministers, Desmond Lardner-Burke and Jack Howman. Nyagumbo, while intrigued by the idea, said he just didn't believe it could be carried off. Sithole pressed on regardless.

In October 1968 he tried to smuggle letters out of Salisbury jail instructing Zanu contacts in Highfields to carry out his assassination orders.

The Reverend Bill Clark was Chaplain General to all prisons in Rhodesia and was one of the very few to have unlimited access to the detainees at the time. In 1980, before the elections, he felt free to talk for the first time about the men he counselled in prison.

'Ndabaningi Sithole, during his years of detention in Salisbury prison, became more and more remote from those of his comrades locked up in the same block,' Clark recalled.

'There were constant murmurings of discontent against his leadership. Party funds into which contributions were paid by various organisations and by devious routes were being held, it was claimed, in several of his private bank accounts.

'Despite the disenchantment with his leadership, he held on to it until he was caught in the act of throwing instructions encased in oranges over the prison wall to members of his party who, by pre-arrangement, assembled as visitors waiting for the gates to be opened. There were also members of the special branch lounging around. They confiscated the oranges. The fruit had been cut out and expertly stuffed with instructions on how Prime Minister Smith was to be assassinated.'

Reverend Clark says that Sithole was then transferred to a cell well away from the others like Mugabe. He sent an urgent message saying Clark had to visit him at once. Clark said the usually aloof Sithole was a changed man.

'The welcome I received was without parallel,' Clark recalls.

'I'll hang for this,' Sithole announced. 'Unless I can do something to form the basis of my defence.'

Sithole wanted to send letters to President Kaunda and Hastings Banda of Malawi, as well as Chitepo in Lusaka.

'They were all along the same lines,' Clark says, 'purporting to convey that he had undergone a change of heart and intention, which meant that he was prepared to dispense with revolutionary tactics and seek his aspirations through peaceful means.'

Sithole was anxious when he finished writing them.

'What do you think?' he asked the chaplain.

Clark said it all seemed rather sudden. He doubted it would have the support of Mugabe and the others.

Sithole told him: 'I am fighting for my life. I must produce something of evidence for my defence. The letters must be put in the hands of the special branch.'

At the end of January 1969 Sithole went on trial charged with conspiring to assassinate Smith. The prosecution claimed he had decided that the *Fearless* proposals meant that the British Government had 'sold out' the Africans and the only way to secure a change of mind on the part of the British was to do something dramatic – like assassinating Ian Smith.

The trial was a sensation, not only for the weird and fanciful plot, but because of what the volte-face Sithole attempted at the end of it all. Found guilty, Sithole told the court: 'My Lord, I wish to publicly disassociate myself in word, thought and deed from any subversive activities, from any terrorist activities and from any form of violence.'

Mugabe, told in his cell of Sithole's statements to the court, expressed dismay at this 'treachery'. Privately he was not too dismayed at all. He now knew Sithole was finished as leader of the party. As Reverend Clark remembers: 'There was much rejoicing among Sithole's erstwhile disciples in the remand section of the prison. They made no effort to hide their glee.

'They made it plain they had got rid of him forever. Robert Mugabe was declared his successor.'

Clark's memories of Mugabe at this time are very clear – he recalls him as a tough, uncompromising leader who grew in stature throughout his years in prison.

'Mugabe,' says Clark, 'was intellectually and academically a man of strong moral fibre and a disciplined sense of purpose. He had long since revealed all the attributes required of a leader ... I had every reason to respect him during the eight years I was privileged to know him.

'He is, without doubt, a horse of true unsurpassed pedigree whom all the other runners recognise as the one most likely to win the election race ... he has been described as the chosen one. He will not be side-tracked from fulfilment of his destiny.

'His emotions remained unruffled in adversity. He will rule and govern with his head.'

Within a few days of Sithole being sentenced to six

years in prison, the executive in prison organised a secret ballot to choose his successor as president of the party. Mugabe won. Now Sithole, isolated from the rest in the maximum security wing, was approached by the head of the special branch, Superintendent Bill Robinson. Robinson got him to agree to a deal whereby he would dissolve Zanu in return for a free passage to the United States, where he could live in exile..

Sithole put the idea to Mugabe and Takawira, hinting they might join him. They expressed amazement mixed with outrage. Mugabe now believed Sithole had been broken completely by the authorities. According to Nyagumbo, Sithole's reaction to their anger was: 'That's all right, you have turned down my constructive suggestion. But I assure you that I am not going to spend all the six years in prison. I am going to extricate myself.'

Sithole's plans to get himself out proved futile. He remained in prison and in March 1973 he rejoined Mugabe and the rest of the executive committee. They had not yet taken any formal decision to remove him from the committee but Mugabe was not the undisputed leader of the men in jail. Sithole once again proposed the disbanding of Zanu: in return he would obtain guarantees for their release.

Some wanted him suspended from the committee. Mugabe, anxious to avoid any split that might become public and so suggest disarray, preferred another tactic. Sithole, he said, was 'beyond the pale'. He was to be frozen out of all contact with anyone.

From 1970 onwards the little good news that Mugabe received came mostly from Mozambique. There wasn't much of it in letters from Sally and friends, but it was enough to tell him what he wanted to know. Frelimo, the Mozambique liberation front, was making slow but steady progress in its war against the Portuguese colonial government. By 1972, their guerrillas were in control of large areas of northern Mozambique. The more they advanced, Mugabe sensed, the greater the freedom for Zanu's own small forces trying to infiltrate along the border. And more likely a Frelimo victory became, the more confident was Mugabe of finding a permanent base for his own war.

It was Christmas that year that Mugabe heard of the first Zanu attack of any real note since the Sinoia incident six years before.

On 21 December a small guerrilla group attacked a farmhouse near Centenary, about forty miles from the Mozambique border. One child was wounded, three others and their grandmother escaped. The farmer moved his family to a neighbouring farm – and two nights later they were attacked there, the farmer and one of his daughters being injured by shrapnel as the guerrillas attacked with rockets and grenades. They withdrew, burning down the farm store and a nearby church. In the morning when an army patrol came to investigate, their truck hit a landmine. One white corporal died, his three companions were injured.

The whites always dated the beginning of the war from that attack in Centenary, just as Zanu always went back to the 'battle of Sinoia'. At either time, neither side realised just how long and bloody it was to be.

South Africa's John Vorster did. For years he'd been talking surreptitiously to President Kaunda in Lusaka, always leaving the door open for negotiations. Vorster had been alarmed at the guerrilla attacks in late 1972. He had good reason to be. With the war in Mozambique intensifying, and the Portuguese will to fight it dying slowly as their casualties mounted, Vorster feared that his country could soon be in the front line. At the same time as he was making overtures to Kaunda about a fresh search for a settlement in Rhodesia, he was re-inforcing Smith's forces in Rhodesia. South Africa's first line defence was Rhodesia's – the Zambezi. Any incursion over that would raise the alarm in Pretoria as quickly as it did in Salisbury. The military coup of General Spinoza in Lisbon in April 1974 changed Vorster's battle-plan overnight. No longer could the Portuguese be relied upon to stand as firm against the guerrillas in Mozambique and Angola now that the generals were in charge in Lisbon, vowing to pull their armies out of Africa and decolonise as soon as possible. No longer was Rhodesia South Africa's front line. Now it was the border with Mozambique. In the circumstances, Vorster realised at once that he could not afford to commit himself or his country to a war in Rhodesia without bringing it to his own front door and so incurring the wrath of his black African neighbours. He now wanted peace at almost any cost: and he was prepared to sacrifice Smith to get it.

Smith remained as obdurate as ever. Sensing yet more winds of change, he said in August that year: 'If it takes one, two or ten years, we are prepared to ride this one out ... settlement is desirable but only on our terms.'

By October Vorster was talking to Kaunda, not directly but through their respective personal aides. Together they worked out the ground-plan for negotiations, Kaunda showing an enthusiasm that belied the economic consequences he had suffered from the closure of his border with Rhodesia in 1973.

For the present they agreed on the immediate release of all political detainees; the end of the state of emergency; and the restoration of legality to Zanu, Zapu and other nationalist parties.

For the future, they drew up a basis for talks: a transition period of five years leading to majority rule: a qualified franchise that was near enough to one man one vote to satisfy Kaunda; and the appointment of Africans to senior posts in both government and the civil service.

Detente was underway. What neither Vorster nor Kaunda nor Nyerere knew was that Mugabe was now the effective leader of Zanu in jail. Smith, from his special branch briefings, did. But he wasn't saying.

He did, however, give Kaunda's aide Mark Chona a typically blunt warning when Chona came to collect the detained nationalists for talks in Lusaka in early November. 'If you can achieve unity,' Smith said wagging a finger at him, 'you can come back and cut this finger off.'

Throughout 1974 the detainees were moved several times. Mugabe stayed in Salisbury, still studying and reading more and more about the situation in Mozambique and the collapse of the dictatorship in Portugal with excitement and fascination. Nyagumbo, Nkala and Tekere were transferred to Que Que. From there they began to urge Mugabe to suspend Sithole. If it did come to talks, they could not afford to be 'saddled' with Sithole as their leader. Mugabe and Malianga were strongly opposed to the idea, according to Nyagumbo. But as word began to filter through from Zambia of 'detente', they recognised the need to move. On 1 November, the executive voted to suspend Sithole.

The timing could not have been more fortunate. The following day they heard for the first time that negotiations were now imminent.

Mugabe, from the first hint of talks, had not only been bitterly opposed to the idea of detente – he also poured scorn on Kaunda for instigating it.

'We wondered,' said Mugabe, 'how Kaunda, a man dedicated to pan-Africanism and to our national cause, could now hobnob with our enemy.'

The Zanu executive in prison rejected the offer of talks as long as they stayed in prison. Kaunda sent Chona to talk them out of that – or rather to persuade Sithole because the Front Line leaders, Kaunda and Nyerere, still believed he was the leader of the party. Sithole did nothing to discourage the idea. Sithole was called in to a prison office to see Chona. Quite by chance Mugabe was sitting yet more exams in the same room. He put down his pen and joined in. Chona produced a letter from Nyerere, Kaunda, Frelimo's Samora Machel and Seretse Khama of Botswana, urging Sithole to come to the talks.

Back in their cells, the executive decided to send Mugabe and Malianga to Lusaka. After all the years in detention, the deprivation, the aching boredom, the humiliation and the fearful loneliness, Mugabe was driven to the airport in a chauffered limousine and put aboard an executive jet. It was to be a brief taste of the other side of Rhodesian political life.

When they arrived in Zambia, Nyerere could barely conceal his anger. Mugabe was not the leader of Zanu, he said. Sithole was. Mugabe and Malianga were promptly dispatched back to Salisbury and jail.

The whole process, Mugabe said on his return to his cell, was a 'sham ... farce'.

In the next few weeks he went along with the talks, knowing that he could so buy his freedom. Sithole re-assumed the mantle of leadership. But it was no more than that, as even the president began to realise.

It was at the end of one shuttle by jet to Lusaka that he saw Sally for the first time in 10 years. She had flown out from London to meet him. It was a total surprise for him, and Sally herself hadn't realised just what a shock it would be. 'I saw him in a flash in the group that arrived from Salisbury,' she says. 'And then I collapsed, I fainted, I went straight out on the floor.'

'The next time I saw Robert was in President Kaunda's private clinic in State House. It was very moving, but there was no time. Two days later they took Robert back to jail in Salisbury.'

Not for long, however. In mid-December Mugabe, along with Nkomo, Sithole and Bishop Abel Muzorewa, was released as Ian Smith announced a ceasefire. But there was no truce in Mugabe's mind as huge crowds gathered in the black townships to welcome them home.

'We had decided to accept detente purely as a tactic to buy the time we needed to organise and intensify the armed struggle,' he said.

In short, detente, in Mugabe's case, was just another word for freedom. Freedom to wage war.

Chapter 4 — Exile

Herbert Chitepo, the chairman of Zanu and commander of the forces, knew his life was in danger.

His fears had been aroused as early as 1973. In September of that year Zanu's bi-annual conference in Lusaka had been marked unmistakably by the personal ambitions of members of the party leadership. There were few political differences among them but the lust for power sought a base by exploiting the ethnic composition of the party, and especially its fighting forces.

A challenge to Chitepo's chairmanship never materialised, but there were radical changes in the composition of the leadership under him at that conference. Zanu had always been predominantly made up of Karanga and Manyika groupings, historically the two rival peoples of the Shona tribe. Now the Karangas, from which the central command of the guerilla force was drawn, secured several key portfolios: finance, information and defence in the form of Josiah Tongogara. The Manyikas, led by Chitepo, were left with his chairmanship, external relations and political commissar.

For the next year the power struggle simmered, then boiled as the Zanu army suffered serious setbacks in the field for lack of ammunition, food and men while following the orders of a new battle-plan conceived by Chitepo and Tongogara after the conference.

'The strategic aim is to attenuate the enemy forces by causing their deployment over the entire country. The subsequent mobilisation of a large number of civilians from industry, business and agriculture would cause serious economic problems. This would have a psychologically devastating effect on the morale of the whites,' Chitepo wrote in November 1973.

The theory made sense, the practice did anything but. By November 1974, at the end of the first year of the new strategy, the Rhodesians were sustaining one loss among their own men for every 10 guerrillas killed. Barely 150 Zanu men remained in the north-east of Rhodesia. By taking the war to the whole of the country, they had spread themselves too thinly and the consequences were disastrous.

The same month there was rebellion. In a Zanu camp at Chifombo on the Zambia–Mozambique border, a group of guerrillas arrested their commanders, took control of the central command, and elected one Thomas Nhari, a law graduate from Salisbury who had joined Zanu five years before, as their leader. All of them were Manyikas and they were quick to denounce Tongogara, a Karanga, for the failures in the field.

On 9 December Nhari arrived in Lusaka with a gang of 20 guerrillas. They abducted Tongogara's wife and brother-in-law, then kidnapped three party leaders: Mukudzei Mudzi, executive secretary; Kumbirai Kangai, welfare secretary, and Henry Hamadziripi, treasurer. The rebel convoy was heading for Tongogara's house when it was spotted by Rugare Gumbo, the information secretary. He called the police and most of the rebels were arrested.

Tongogara was despatched to the front to crush the rebellion. Early in the New Year he stormed the camp at Chifombo: 45 people were killed. His own forces regained control.

On 22 January a committee of three, headed by Chitepo, tried the rebels at Chifombo. Those convicted – it took a matter of minutes for some – were executed a few hundred yards from the hearings. That wasn't the only summary justice meted out. Convinced in their own minds that the Manyika group had started the rebellion against them, the Karanga faction launched a wave of kidnappings and executions. Some were murdered in

Mozambique, others in Zambia. More than a hundred were killed.

The conspiracy, in the eyes of the hunters, had to lead to Chitepo, and his position was rapidly becoming untenable. Some of his friends had been executed under his authority, now supporters who had survived accused him of betraying them and the Manyika element. The Karanga group believed he had been behind the rebellion to remove Tongogara.

During January and February, Tongogara's men assumed effective control of the party. Chitepo was by this time little more than a figurehead. On 16 March he told President Kaunda that Zanu was no longer under his control: his own life was in danger, he said. When Kaunda asked him 'who was threatening him', he replied: Tongogara and Hamadziripi.

Some 36 hours later, as Chitepo was starting his car up at his house in Lusaka, a bomb exploded inside the vehicle. It killed him instantly.

The murder created serious disarray in both the army and the party. Tongogara fled to Mozambique, his allies to Tanzania. Kaunda was furious and promised 'no stone unturned' in the hunt for the assassins.

Within two weeks of the murder, he announced a special international commission to investigate it comprising of officials from 14 African States. It took them a year to reach their findings. Tongogara was returned by Mozambique and was found guilty.

According to the commission, the Zanu high command under Tongogara's chairmanship authorised the murder two days before. The involvement of Smith, or the Zambians was ruled out.

Tongogara, to the day of his own death, was to deny the charge.

At the time he accused Smith, Vorster and Kaunda, insisting that Chitepo stood between them and the success of their policy of detente. Mugabe was later to agree. 'I think it is an act done through or by direct participation of the Zambian government,' he said in 1976.

Indeed on the day before his own death in December 1979, Tongogara asked Samora Machel: 'Do you believe I killed anyone?'

The President answered 'No.'

Tongogara said: 'I'm pleased about that.'

Nevertheless, it was to leave a lasting scar on both Zanu and Tongogara in particular. Imprisoned for 18 months, he was to be behind bars at the very time the party and army needed drastic reorganisation and was craving new leadership.

Chitepo's wife Victoria said at his funeral that the struggle for Zimbabwe would not stop with the death of one man. Indeed it did not.

And in the vacuum left by Chitepo's murder and Tongogara's imprisonment, Mugabe was to emerge as the main, if not the unchallenged, leader of both army and party.

For Mugabe, enjoying some rare freedom in Salisbury, the death of Chitepo combined with the trial of Sithole to convince him that he had only one option: to flee to Mozambique.

Sithole had been charged, just a week after the assasination in Lusaka, with leading an unlawful organisation, namely Zanu. The trial was 11 days old when Vorster stepped in to tell Ian Smith that it could only damage the chances of peace. Smith backed down very reluctantly and within 24 hours Sithole was on his way to a summit with Nkomo and Muzorewa in Tanzania.

By now, Mugabe was not just suspicious of the peace-makers, he was positively contemptuous. Smith, and Vorster, were simply leading Nkomo, Muzorewa and Sithole into a sell-out of the Africans. It wouldn't work, he insisted, because the true Zanu, his Zanu, would never accept it.

First of all, though, he had to establish himself as the

undisputed leader of the party. That was not possible in Rhodesia, where he was liable to arrest at any moment. Now, with the death of Chitepo and Kaunda's ensuing fury, it would not be possible in Zambia either.

By mid-April Mugabe and Edgar Tekere were ready to leave. They had enough evidence to suggest that they could expect hundreds of guerrilla volunteers to follow if they made the move. They, like other detainees released in December, had been on secret recruiting drives in their own home areas. The recruits would need training camps and homes in Mozambique.

Tekere's commitment to Mugabe was unstinting. 'Then, as now, I loved Mugabe,' he was to recall three years later in Mozambique. 'I owed so much to him. He had taught me so much, he had made me study during all the years in detention.

'He educated me about myself and the struggle. I had no doubts about going with him. there was no other way.'

They couldn't go freely, they had to escape. In the end they literally walked out of Rhodesia. Mugabe was to make it across the hills into Mozambique in secret, the same way across the same hills his men were to attack in the years to come. By car and by foot they reached the border within a few days. Then they stopped at the Nyafuru agriculture co-operative a few miles short of the border.

A community of about 3,000 tribespeople had been fighting their own war with the Smith government for years. Chief Rekayi Tangwena had ancestors buried on the land dating back to well before the arrival of the first white settlers. But that meant little to the Smith government. Their lands were in the half of the country apportioned to the white community and they were squatters, the government said. The bulldozers moved in to knock down the mud huts, the people took to the hills, eventually they formed a co-operative with the help of British missionaries.

Mugabe was fascinated by it. He and Tekere spent two weeks there, 'two of the most educational weeks of my life', Mugabe later recalled. They rested, they read, they watched the co-operative farm at work. A group of Tangwena tribesmen smuggled them across the border one night in late April. The route they took was not the easiest way into the areas controlled by the Frelimo army of Mozambique. But it took them, at Mugabe's insistence, into the zones where Zanla guerrillas were based and operating. Some of the guerrillas he met along the way had been sent to Mozambique after his own clandestine recruiting meetings in Rhodesia in the previous few months. Meeting these men again was crucial to Mugabe, enabling him to show an interest in and relationship with the army he was trying to lead.

Within weeks seven senior tribesmen were given prison sentences for helping people, including Mugabe, to escape. Hardly surprising that chief Tangwena and hundreds of his tribespeople were among the first to follow Mugabe. And among the first to come back after independence Chief Tangwena returned to Nyafuru in triumph in June 1980. Mugabe had arrived in Mozambique just two months before Machel was to take power. The war there was over and, for the moment, the president-designate was involved in the immediate problems of a country adjusting slowly to peace.

The two men met for the first time. Machel doubted Mugabe's ability to lead Zanu and, furthermore, he had no time for the kind of rivalry and squabbling that had led to Chitepo's death. It made him deeply suspicious of his newest resident, before he met him. That was to change the minute he did.

The two were worlds apart in terms of background and development. Machel the warrior-president whose school had been the bush war of Frelimo; Mugabe the quiet, academic revolutionary whose education had been based on his reading in prison.

One strong leader recognised another. Each appreciated the other's qualities. It was not quite the attraction of opposites, rather an uncanny, indefinable sense they both had of complementing each other.

Still, Machel at this stage was in no position to offer Mugabe anything more than a safe harbour. In addition, the Mozambican leader wanted clear proof that Mugabe was the undisputed leader of his party and, more importantly for Machel, his army. Machel was convinced that the future leader of Zimbabwe would emerge from the ranks of the fighting forces, as he had done. He was not yet convinced Mugabe was the man.

As a result, he put Mugabe 'under wraps', placing him in a house in the port city of Quelimane. It wasn't quite house arrest, but Mugabe wasn't entirely free to move either.

The months that followed were some of the loneliest in Mugabe's whole life: they were also arguably some of the most important, because it was now that he had the opportunity to establish himself as leader, to consolidate that 'vote' in prison.

He needed permission to travel, but he did so frequently. To the burgeoning guerrilla and refugee camps in the northern provinces; to Tanzania to set up the training camps that were to be the springboard for the war from here on; to make the first tentative overtures for the foreign support he knew he would need.

As Nkomo, Sithole, and Muzorewa pursued detente with Smith through Vorster during 1975 – culminating in the abortive attempt at a settlement at Victoria Falls in August that year – Mugabe was carefully nurturing his personal standing with the Zanu army. He wasn't entirely comfortable with the role of guerrilla leader but no one who heard his impassioned advocacy of the armed struggle in any of his numerous visits to the camps doubted his commitment. And judging by the number coming over the border into Mozambique, he knew he was winning his own battle to create his own power base. Within six months of leaving Rhodesia, he had about 10,000 refugees following him, many of them fit for an army. The point was not lost on Ian Smith and his army commander, Peter Walls. It brought them more readily to the negotiating table with the ANC than ever before.

Mugabe's strategy had been based on the premise that Smith would never concede enough to get any one of Sithole, Muzorewa or Nkomo in on a settlement. He was right. The failure at Victoria Falls had finally persuaded the Front Line presidents, particularly Kaunda and Nyerere, that there was no alternative but war. All they needed, like Machel, was proof of Mugabe's credentials.

It wasn't long in coming. In October dozens of officers at Mgagao, the largest Zanu camp in Tanzania, issued a bitter denunciation of Muzorewa, Sithole and James Chikerema, the men who might have liked now to have claimed the guerrillas of Zanu as their own.

'These three have proved to be completely hopeless and ineffective as leaders of the Zimbabwe revolution,' the officers wrote in a memorandum to the OAU, and the governments of Tanzania and Mozambique. 'They have done everything to hamper the struggle through their own power struggle. They have no interest in the revolution or the people at heart, but only their personal interests. They cherish an insatiable lust for power.' They added: 'Robert Mugabe is the only man who can act as middle man.'

The collapse of detente at Victoria Falls had also spawned a truce and pact between Nkomo's army in Zapu and Zanu. In November, after weeks of patient negotiations between the two, a new army was formed. The title was the Zimbabwe People's army, ZIPA, its high command an 18-man council with nine representatives from each.

Because Zanu had many more men in the field, it

provided the commander in the burly frame of Rex Nhongo, just 27 but already proven as a guerrilla leader. Tongogara, from his jail in Zambia, had to sanction his appointment. He was also asked, discreetly by Machel, if he supported Mugabe. The answer was yes.

Now the arms that Mugabe needed began to come through, not so much a flood, more a trickle. But enough to give him the firepower to at least prove more than just an irritant to Smith and Walls.

Russian rifles and ammunition, originally destined for Nkomo's Zapu units, began to arrive through Mozambican ports. Mugabe widened his net to get Chinese weapons as well.

The New Year of 1976 saw the first major infiltration on any scale from Mozambique – nearly a thousand guerrillas, many of them raw and fresh from training camps in Tanzania, trying to inveigle themselves as surreptitiously as possible into the Tribal trust lands all along the eastern border, where they could expect support from local tribes that had close ties with the Mozambicans. The tactics were much the same as always. They still attacked white farms and stores; so too was the result. The security forces still claimed many dead for every one of theirs. But now the battle-plan of Tongogara and Chitepo, of spreading the war as far and wide as possible to undermine white morale, had to be taken seriously because of the weight of numbers on the guerrilla side.

The effect was just what Tongogara and Chitepo had hoped for. The call-up was stepped up, the Rhodesians increased their forces by 50 per cent, every man under 38 was forced into duty.

In February 1976 Mugabe had the Front Line presidents in his new adopted home town. Machel, Nyerere, Kaunda and Seretse Khama of Botswana came to Quelimane for a summit. Nkomo told them that his negotiations with Smith – the final attempt at detente – had little chance of success. Mugabe, sitting patiently on the sidelines, knew that he was bound to be the main beneficiary.

Kaunda's warning was clear at the end of the meeting. The patience of the Front Line States with Smith was exhausted. The West had failed them by failing to back their bid for peace. He offered only the bleak prospect of war and, implicitly, the Marxism of men like Mugabe.

'The worst they have feared all along – the factor of Communism – must now inevitably be introduced in Zimbabwe because majority rule must now be decided on the battlefield,' he said.

Peter Walls was quick to reply. 'We will not be pushed around or surrender to any Marxist-inspired land grab,' he said. 'We are going to fight.'

All that Mugabe needed was Machel's backing. He got it at Quelimane and when, days later, the Rhodesian Air Force attacked a village just inside Mozambique, the president went a step further. He closed the border with Rhodesia and put his young revolution on a war footing.

More importantly, he gave Mugabe his permission and full support for the northern province of Tete to be used as the base for military strike on Rhodesia.

But Mugabe recognised all too clearly that he needed friends in the outside world too. The following month he travelled to Switzerland, to Zurich, the first time abroad as the recognised leader of Zanu.

It was a major challenge for him and it came at a time of great uncertainty. Yes, he had established himself within the party but the ease of a 'military leader' eluded him. That title belonged to Tongogara, and he was in jail in Zambia. The chances of Zipa holding together were slim, the suspicions about each other in both forces ran too deep.

Furthermore, he was in poor health – Quelimane was at the best of times an unpleasantly humid environment – and he was tired of it. En route to Europe he stopped off in Ghana to see his son's grave. As always, that was to touch him deeply.

He did not have much success in raising money or support in Zurich, despite the fact that everyone who met him was impressed not only by the quality of his intellect but also his commitment to his cause.

Then, towards the end of his stay, a Zanu support organisation called 'Kampfendes Afrika' ('Fighting Africa') presented him with 10,000 Swiss francs. It was the first large contribution he had ever received on behalf of his party and it made a great impression on him. It was precisely the boost he needed, the money in itself was not as important as the commitment it represented to him.

The little girl who actually gave him the money at a small ceremony in Zurich was not forgotten. Four years later Mugabe was to make sure that she was invited to Independence celebrations. Many of the leaders, ambassadors and diplomats at the receptions in Salisbury wondered aloud just who the child was as she was given the same status and treatment as them, including the occasional hug from the prime minister-elect. She was the little girl from Zurich, a symbol of the days when he was short of friends.

On his return to Quelimane, Mugabe felt sufficiently secure to now begin to put his stamp on the party, its philosophy and policy. On 15 April he issued a memorandum to all Zanu offices and members. Its humble origin was reflected in the address at the top, 'PO Box 279, Quelimane, Mozambique.' It began: 'Dear Comrades, Congratulations! Zanu is once again in its full revolutionary stride.'

It continued: 'As you are all well aware, for nearly a whole year after 7 December 1974, Zanu battled for survival against the most tremendous of odds posed by the wily architects of detente. In the wake of that struggle, some of our weak-kneed comrades chose the softer road to capitulation rather than walk the gruelling path to protracted war.

'Indeed, we have seen no less person than the Commander-in-chief (Sithole) of our Zanla forces perform an unprecedented dramatic and counter-revolutionary feat as he somersaulted to a disgraceful surrender, deserting, thereby, the very Forces he had helped to build. In the process, he joined cause with the enemy ... and thus became an unmitigated traitor to the whole revolution.

'An ordinary Zanu member may, in these circumstances, justifiably ask, 'Comrade, but if gold rusts, what will iron do?' Our reply is quite simple. True gold never rusts. We have had a deception. We mistook brass for gold.

'The one is a low quality metal, varies with circumstance and is a king to expediency: the other is a high-quality metal, defies change and circumstance and is as constant as principle.'

Having asserted the quality of his claim to power, Mugabe turns to re-organisation of the party under his leadership. The make-up, the functions, the duties of regional committees and their sub-committees (including ones for health, social services and education) are all spelt out.

All the questions raised are answered.

'It will be noticed,' writes Mugabe, 'that in formulating the organisational plan Zambia is excluded, although Zanu's external membership is greatest there. The reason is clearly that Zambia is still hostile territory. The Zanu organs there, nevertheless, continue to operate quite effectively, albeit under one cover or another. Our task forces must, therefore, be found in North America, the United Kingdom and Europe where our next greatest external following is to be found.'

Finally, he turns to the military and the war. Here his ground is shaky, Mugabe is still grasping for support and control of the Zanu army. He knows that Nkomo, by now in control of the ANC, and Sithole, trying to get an external wing of the ANC called the Zimbabwe Liberation Council (ZILC) off the ground, have visited the camps in Mozambique, Tanzania and Zambia in the past few months.

Mugabe is as uncompromising and scathing as he believes the guerrillas want him to be.

'Let me seize this opportunity to clear one issue which continues to cause concern. The break between Zanu–Zanla and ANC–ZLC is complete. The Army will NEVER, NEVER, NEVER come under the interfering hand of the ZLC.

'It has been necessary for us to allow members of a small Zapu army to join our forces so that the possibility of a second army developing disappears. But the requirement from us is that they must divorce themselves completely from Nkomo and his counter-revolutionary approach.

'There is, therefore, a joint military front between Zanu and Zapu, but only at the fighting level and no other ... there should not be any mix-up on this matter. There is nothing more than a joint military front with Zapu in which we have the majority of the forces involved.'

He ends this first message to the comrades with a subtle blend of courtesy and firmness.

'Please let us have your suggestions, if any, for the improvement of the re-organisational plan. If you have none, please get the organs on to the war-path, and implement the schemes without waiting for further instructions from us.

Yours in the Struggle

R. G. Mugabe

Secretary-General Zanu.'

It was his first and last memorandum from Quelimane. That spring he travelled frequently to Maputo, where the president allocated the Mugabes a small but pleasant

87

Portuguese-style villa at the end of a road of terraced houses just off the coast road. Avenida Dona Maria Segunda, one of the few Portuguese road names to survive anywhere in Mozambique, was to be their home for the next four years. Sally, with her flair for making the most out of little, quickly turned it into home. Chickens were soon running in the backyard, she settled into cooking once again, and Mugabe at last felt he could build himself a base. An office followed, in a high-rise block in the suburb of Pollona, the fashionable, diplomatic area of Maputo. It was hardly perfect; Russian trade specialists were on the floors above and below Zanu. But it was a start.

From the word go, Mugabe's relations with the Russians in Maputo were at best frosty, at worst furious. The Soviet Union had already chosen its 'man' for Zimbabwe, and that was Joshua Nkomo. Over the next three years Mugabe would talk to them time and again, seeking hardware for his army but careful to insist there would be no strings attached.

Always he got the same response from the Russians. He, Mugabe, would have to admit that Nkomo was number one in the nationalist leadership. At one point, when the Russians did offer him arms, they demanded written admissions from Mugabe that he would recognise Nkomo as leader. Mugabe, incensed, refused to go any further. Instead he turned more and more to the Chinese. By the middle of 1976 he was forging the kind of commitment to Peking that raised the inevitable question of what they would demand in return.

Mugabe was quick to deny that the support made him a servant of China.

'Our war could not be waged without the assistance of China. But the Chinese have never attached any conditions to their supply of weapons ... there is an understanding between the Chinese and us that we are free to choose our friends and pursue any policy which we thought best suited for our country.

'Because we get arms from them, it doesn't mean that we are married to them.'

He added: 'We will not give in to any pressure to abandon our Chinese friends. They are very good to us.'

He was a regular visitor to most of the Western embassies, most of whom were desperate to give their governments a fuller picture of the man who was building his base in Mozambique. Mugabe, polite yet tenacious in telling them what he thought, was to make a lasting first impression on almost all of them.

'My immediate feeling about him was that he far and away outstripped every other nationalist leader,' recalled one Western diplomat who met him then. 'I remember thinking that this is the man who ought to be running Rhodesia.'

It was a view shared by New York congressman Stephen Sollarz, one of the very few Western politicians to see Mugabe in Mozambique during the first year there. Sollarz, on a fact-finding mission through Southern Africa, was surprised from what he heard about Mugabe that he agreed to see him in Quelimane at the end of his enforced stay there.

'He impressed me then, as he does now, as one of the most able leaders on the African continent,' said Sollarz after Mugabe's election in 1980. 'The most striking thing about him was his intelligence and sophistication, the way he was so receptive to all ideas and points of view whether they were coming from Peking, Moscow or Washington. He certainly didn't strike me as a fanatic.'

Sollarz was also struck by the way Mugabe put his party before himself. 'He was very candid and it was clear there had been divisions among his people. But he said again and again that he put the integrity and the unity of Zanu above everything else.'

With Chinese support, the war was stepped up. As the Mugabes were moving to Maputo, more than 500 men were infiltrated across the border. That was in April. In June a further 300 were dispatched. The guerrillas were still pinned in the border areas but as training and organisation improved, so too did the results. Now for the first time they succeeded in subverting the local population. In the sugar and wheat-growing country around Chiredzi and Chipinga, they started issuing orders to plantation workers to stay away from work: if they were disobeyed, they ambushed company buses en route to work. They mined the roads, even used mortars on mills and pumping stations.

The reply from Salisbury was a further call-up. And then, in August, the first large-scale raid into Mozambique itself.

There had been hit and run strikes in the months before and by the time the Rhodesians attacked a camp at Nyazonia, about 35 miles from the border, they were well rehearsed. They advanced in convoy, wearing Frelimo uniforms, with Frelimo insignia on their trucks, even singing Frelimo songs. Hundreds of the refugees in the camp – there were also about 700 guerrillas – gathered to welcome them.

It was then they opened fire.

Smith said it was a guerrilla training camp. Mugabe and Machel insisted it wasn't.

The United Nations envoy sent to investigate told the press that 670 refugees – he repeated the word refugees – had been killed.

Henry Kissinger's plans for a whirlwind peace in Rhodesia were, in Mugabe's view, doomed from the start. The fact that he had cajoled, persuaded, finally pushed Ian Smith into accepting 'majority rule' (Smith would not accept 'black majority rule') did not even begin to make Mugabe believe that the whites would make the

kind of wholesale compromises that had been the basis
on which he had argued and won support among the
army.

The Kissinger shuttles back and forth across Southern
Africa in mid-1976 did, however, enable Mugabe to
emerge as the internationally recognised leader of Zanu.
The Front Lines States, willing at least to entertain the
mercurial American secretary of state, tried to resolve
the divisions and differences among the nationalists
before any peace conference started. From their own
soundings, the Front Line presidents now knew Mugabe
had the support and confidence of most of the Zanu
guerrillas and Zipa units. They rejected Sithole absolutely, they viewed Nkomo with suspicion and a degree
of loathing for his negotiations with Smith in the months
before.

That left the Zapu forces loyal to Nkomo isolated and
threatened. Already they had clashed with Zanu men in
camps in Tanzania, they fled when they should have been
integrated under the Zipa banner and the leadership of
Rex Nhongo.

In September, the Front Line presidents called
Mugabe, Nkomo, Sithole and Muzorewa to Dar-es-
Salaam. If the presidents had hoped to bring them all
together, it was an unqualified failure. Mugabe and
Nkomo did not even attempt to reconcile their differences. Mugabe, in particular, was scathing about Nkomo,
accusing him of pulling Zapu out of the war and allowing
Zanu–Zipa to carry the battle and the losses alone. Sithole
withdrew from the ANC, and said he would form his
own independent Zanu. Muzorewa left for Rhodesia in
the hopes of being the one nationalist with a base back
home.

Three weeks later Smith made his historic address to
the nation accepting the principle of majority rule – and
offered the 'opportunity we have never had before – an
offer to Rhodesians to work out amongst themselves,

without interference from outside, our future.'

All the parties were now bound for the conference table. Or were they? Just three days after the Smith declaration Mugabe, talking to guerrillas in Zambia, appeared to torpedo that idea. From his point of view, he saw nothing to be gained by attending. The Kissinger plan effectively left the whites in control – in control of the army, in control of the police, in fact still in power.

In the wake of the failure at the conference in Geneva, Mugabe was to get more than his share of blame for his apparent refusal to compromise and his attempts to undermine the credibility of the conference before it had even started.

The fact is that Mugabe believed wholeheartedly at this stage in the armed struggle as the only means of bringing Smith to real negotiations. And Mugabe was still seeking to shore up his own credibility with the guerrillas, realising that without their loyalty and faith he would never be in a position to force any worthwhile concessions from Smith.

'What is required,' he told the geurrillas on 27 September 'is the total destruction of Smith's army and immediate replacement by Zanu forces ... we shouldn't worry about the Kissinger–British proposals. They can put in any puppet government they want, but a puppet government cannot contain us.'

Now, in their desperation to find a united nationalist front, the Front Line tried to marry Nkomo and Muzorewa. It might have worked had not the two of them been eaten up by jealousy of each other. They both returned to Salisbury to talk to their supporters about an alliance. Muzorewa got home to a huge crowd, a few hundred turned out for Nkomo. As always, they measured their popularity in terms of the numbers who came out for them. Muzorewa, accordingly, felt he didn't need Nkomo. Now there was only one way out for Nkomo, he would have to come to terms with Mugabe.

If not, he stood to lose both his army and the support of the Front Line. President Nyerere brought the two together in Dar-es-Salaam at the beginning of October. They spent seven long days talking and on 9 October announced the alliance. They called it the Patriotic Front. There was no common philosophy, strategy or even the bond of trust and friendship. Convenience and expediency dictated.

Together they issued demands for the Geneva conference: the lifting of restrictions on political parties inside Rhodesia, the cessation of political trials, freedom for political prisoners and the integration of Smith's delegation so it was reduced to being an 'arm' of the British team in Geneva.

At this stage, they came to no firm agreement on the conduct of the war apart from agreeing to fight together, and Mugabe insisting that Nkomo throw more men into the field. Privately, Mugabe was not concerned that Nkomo's men were better trained, that the Zapu high command was arguably more organised. He felt that he was one step ahead of Nkomo in that his men would be better qualified and more adept at winning and minds, which in the end he knew would count. Mugabe's confidence about handling Nkomo was decisive in making him accept the alliance when it was suggested. And he was to be proved right. As two armies in the field, Zipra (Nkomo) was a much more disciplined, effective force than Zanla (Mugabe), which was twice Zipra's size. But Zipra was a poor rival when it came to setting up party committees and cadres in the 'liberated zones'.

Mugabe went to Geneva as the unknown factor. Kissinger had not met him, the British had carefully nurtured a relationship with him through the embassy in Maputo but he was still reported to be intensely suspicious of their intentions. He accepted copies of the London *Times* from embassy staff, which he read avidly, but he refused to allow relations to move beyond the cordial and polite.

When he and his delegation were called to the embassy to be given their tickets to Geneva, they said they could not accept them as some were first-class (for Mugabe, Muzenda and two others). What followed was a curious wrangle in which the tickets had to be turned in and the money used to send more delegates, all of them economy class.

It was typical of the way relations between Mugabe and the British were haunted by misinterpretation of each other's motives.

As such Mugabe remained inscrutable. And when the West turned to the records of the man, they found only bald statements of militancy that did not augur well for Geneva. Yet well before this Mugabe had opened the way to compromise.

'Yes, we are Marxist–Leninists,' he said in an interview earlier in the year. 'The main principles of socialism do not vary but the application varies. In our particular circumstances you have about five million people in the rural areas, the peasants, and about one million in other areas. You have got to take into account their own receptive customs and the economic situation which has been established by the settlers.

'You can't, you see, bring a set formula to the situation in Zimbabwe overnight.'

When the Patriotic Front was unveiled, President Machel was photographed with Mugabe and Nkomo. The pictures appeared in the papers in Mozambique, the radio reported every word of it. At last, after 18 months, Mugabe had won the full acceptance and backing of his host.

On 18 October Mugabe arrived in Lusaka for pre-conference talks with Nkomo on board the president's plane. At once there was a row with the Front Line States

Wedding Day, February 1961 in the Salisbury township of Harare.
(Sunday Times)

Mugabe shortly after his release from prison after eleven years in detention, December 1974. *(Gary Woodhouse, Camera Press)*

Nkomo and Mugabe, 'The Patriotic Front', arrive for the Geneva Conference, October 1976. *(Sunday Times)*

Mugabe, the unknown nationalist, meets the world's Press for the first time, in Geneva, October 1976. *(Associated Press)*

Mugabe and Nkomo fielding questions after a stormy meeting with the British at Geneva, November 1976. *(Popperfoto)*

In exile – Mugabe with Simon Muzenda, his deputy (on Mugabe's left) and ZANU office workers in Maputo, Mozambique 1977. *(Sunday Times)*

'One of the stopping points on a life in exile' – Mugabe addressing a Press conference, in Rome, November 1978. *(Popperfoto)*

Mugabe says 'No' to British peace proposals and leaves Lancaster House in defiant mood, November 1979. *(Neil Libbert)*

'Lord Carrington can go to hell' – Mugabe addressing the press conference on the deadlock at Lancaster House talks, November 1979. *(Neil Libbert)*

'I will talk about everything except the Lancaster House agreement' – Mugabe signs for peace, December 1979. From left to right: Muzorewa, Carrington, Gilmour, Nkomo, Mugabe. *(Frank Herrmann, Sunday Times)*

Mugabe, at home in Maputo, talks to author David Smith just before his return to Salisbury, January 1980. *(ITN)*

Back after five years – Mugabe leads his homecoming rally at Zimbabwe Grounds, 27 January 1980. *(Hagar Shour, Camera Press)*

over whether or not Sithole should be allocated a place in Geneva. He claimed one as a right. Nyerere felt he should have one. Mugabe was contemptuous. 'He is a reverend herring, if you pardon the pun,' he said. 'He has left the party.' At the end of the day, Sithole was invited.

In his meeting with Nkomo, the two men agreed on a degree of co-operation and consultation that would have been unthinkable even just a few days before.

When they arrived in Geneva, Mugabe at once seized the initiative. Asked what kind of Rhodesia he wanted, he replied: 'What I am saying is that we are socialist and we shall draw on the socialist systems of Mozambique and Tanzania. One cannot get rid of all the trappings of free enterprise. After all, even the Russians and China have their petit bourgeoisie.

'But in Zimbabwe none of the white exploiters will be allowed to keep an acre of their land.'

That, combined with leaks to the press that Mugabe had told his delegation en route that their aim was 'to destroy the forces of Smith', gave Mugabe the image of the 'bloodthirsty ogre' that was to haunt him thoughout the Geneva talks.

But whatever the labels, like Ian Smith's suggestion that he was 'riding around on cloud nine in a camouflage uniform', Geneva was to provide another vital opportunity for Mugabe to assert his control of the party. His decision, just before it opened, to request the release of Tongogara and the others held in Zambia was a bold one, reflecting his new-found confidence. Tongogara, who arrived offering bland war-like statements such as 'Smith is my enemy', was now in Mugabe's debt. Out of circulation for 18 months, he owed him allegiance and support. And while in the following year, Tongogara may have entertained thoughts of a rebellion against Mugabe's leadership, he was never to forget that Mugabe had made his release a prime requisite in agreeing to go to Geneva.

The conference spluttered and almost collapsed even before it started. Nkomo and Mugabe pushed the demands they had made when the Patriotic Front was formed a fortnight earlier. And Mugabe's team was bitterly critical of Ivor Richard, the British chairman, even to his face.

Mukudzei Mudzi, one of those freed with Tongogara, told Richard in a meeting on the eve of the opening: 'You think we are just a lot of damned niggers.'

When, at the last minute, the Patriotic Front objected that Richard was simply not senior enough to be in the chair, even the British confessed to dismay. They withdrew it, but the air of hostility, suspicion and hate was so strong that the prospects for a settlement had already been damaged beyond repair.

The first obstacle was the interim period leading to independence. Smith, sticking firmly to the Kissinger plan which carried inherent protection for the whites, insisted he had agreed on two years. Mugabe said it had to be 12 months.

They agreed only to disagree. That took a month. Then none of the parties could agree on what form the interim government should take.

In conference, Mugabe sometimes seemed to enjoy himself hugely, his flair for debate and argument developing all the time as his opponents and the British recognised the quality of his advocacy. Privately, he was ready to go home within days of the conference opening. He thought it was a waste of time and money. Only pressure from Nyerere and Kaunda kept him there through the disagreement over the date for independence. He worried about the financial cost to Zanu and ordered his delegation out of their expensive hotels into smaller guest houses. Despite Mugabe's insistence on simple meals cooked by themselves and other cost-cutting devices, Zanu ended up leaving Geneva 10,000 francs in debt to hotels. Mugabe left party officials behind to try to raise the money from sympathetic groups. Finally, the Swiss Government stepped in and paid the bill.

For the first time he was on the world stage – the daily press conferences, the crowd of reporters waiting outside his hotel and the conference hall, the endless requests from newspapers and television for interviews. It didn't so much bother him as amaze him. He realised that from now on he could no longer enjoy the privacy he had always cherished.

In the final weeks of the conference he took to getting up very early, about 5 o'clock for an hour of yoga, meditation and exercises. Then he would go for long walks while the rest of the city slept. He relished the opportunity to wander unnoticed through the centre of the city, stopping to window-shop at the expensive stores. It was, he said, his one chance of the day to be inconscpicuous.

After five weeks, Rex Nhongo, commander of Zipa, flew in to join the Mugabe delegation. A few days later a fire broke out in his hotel room. Nhongo woke Tongogara and others staying in the same block and they escaped unhurt. The cause of the fire was never discovered. Zanu suggested it was a Rhodesian plot, the Rhodesians hinted darkly that it was factional rivalry within Zanu. Within a few weeks of the collapse of the conference, they had reason to think they were right.

After the conference, Tongogara set about re-establishing his authority. Zipa had got nowhere, the armies of Zanu and Zapu continuing to fight each other wherever they met. It still existed in theory, but in fact it was just another name for Zanu's army.

Three men in the Zipa high command stood in Tongogara's way. First Nhongo; then Dzinashe Machingura, a young Marxist extremist who had taught economics in Zambia and was more of a theoretician than a soldier; finally Elias Hondo, an experienced guerrilla who had been in the Front Line since the late 1960s.

97

Even before the Geneva conference and Tongogara's release, they had posed the first serious challenge to Mugabe's assumed leadership. They rejected the Geneva conference in toto, even the idea of going. They feared that Mugabe, whom they viewed as a moderate, would inevitably be drawn into a settlement that would exclude the guerrillas. In September 1976, Machingura implicitly rejected Mugabe while speaking on Maputo radio. 'We do not identify ourselves with any one of the factions trying to lead us,' he said.

There was more to it than that. Machingura was strongly pro-Chinese and had built up a following among Maoist groups at the 'Chitepo college' in Chimoio, northern Mozambique, where military trained cadres of above-average ability were given intensive political courses. They were unhappy about Mugabe's repeated attempts, without success, to offset Zanu's shortage of arms. Even before Geneva there were plans to close the college.

Nhongo and the Machingura group, the dissidents as they became known, came to Geneva under Mugabe's banner very reluctantly. There they found that Mugabe and Tongogara had formed a political-military alliance. In return for supreme military command, Tongogara promised Mugabe his full support as party leader. Machel was informed and was privately delighted.

By the time the dissidents got home, they found themselves isolated. The president had given them free access to Maputo radio, now it was cut off, within a few weeks the entire Machingura group, about 90 in all, were arrested on the orders of Machel. Among them were some high-ranking Zanu members: James Myikadzinashe, deputy director of security and intelligence; and Mugabe's brother-in-law – Marxist economist Dr Sam Geza. Nearly 100 'dissidents' in the campus in Tanzania were also detained.

The war was going badly, an offensive timed to

coincide with Geneva had been a disaster. The threat to his leadership had made Mugabe realise more clearly than ever that the key to the door of power ultimately would lie with those who commanded the guerrillas. Determined not to lose their support, he heeded the warning in Machingura's complaint about the lack and quality of weapons. In May he publicly castigated the OAU at their summit for failing to provide sufficient aid and arms to his army, in July he was in Peking with Tongogara underlining the urgency of his needs. There he used the quiet, forceful powers of persuasion that had already become his hallmark with those he saw as friends. He would never be seen to be begging, and he always stressed the independence of his leadership and his party.

Sally was now involving herself in the job of consolidating their position. She travelled to the guerrilla and refugee camps in northern Mozambique and Tanzania, spending days listening to the problems they had about the shortages of food, clothing and medicine they faced. Before long, she too was going abroad in search of support. She visited the Scandinavian countries regularly, especially Sweden, giving emotional and moving accounts of the refugees' plight based on her own first-hand experience. She proved to be an accomplished fund-raiser as well as an articulate advocate of the Zanu cause.

It was now noticeable that Mugabe sought to inject a touch of military discipline into his routine. In his office in the Avenida Lenin in Maputo, he became something of the commander, his helpers and aides rather like sub-alterns. They would click their heels or stamp a foot to attention when they went to see him. His colleagues on the Central Committee now called him 'Chef', Portuguese for chief. If not, it was 'Comrade', a title he prefers even today as prime minister.

The embryonic rebellion of Machingura also raised the question of security. In 1977, a Zanu office worker was killed in the offices in Maputo when he opened a letter bomb. It was so powerful that it all but demolished the room he was in. Coming as it did, just a few months after Nkomo's key military adviser Jason Moyo was assassinated by a parcel bomb in Lusaka, it forced the entire reorganisation of security and intelligence in Maputo. Mugabe did not move anywhere without bodyguards. There was a guard on his front gate, another at the front door. He asked the Mozambicans to supply an x-ray machine to check all mail. It never came, and a room set aside to store letters and parcels quickly filled to overflowing. At one point, the government said Zanu would just have to dump the packages in the sea. The party helpers refused, and they gingerly started opening the parcels for the much-needed clothing and books inside. It was only in April 1979 that they got an x-ray machine from the Danish Government.

With Tongogara back in command the war, in his own words began to 'bite'. The attacks were more selective, designed to leave the whites in no doubt about the precariousness of their situation if they remained. In February seven missionaries were killed by Zanu guerrillas at St Paul's mission, Musami, little more than 25 miles from the centre of Salisbury. In August a bomb exploded in a store in Salisbury itself, killing 11 and injuring 76 others. The indiscriminate nature of the killing of innocent civilians was not so much defended by Zanu – they knew it couldn't be – but rationalised as the only way of bringing Smith to his knees.

It marked a new stage in the war, there was no longer any examination of ethics or principle. Both the whites and the Africans suffered. Hundreds of schools in the tribal trustlands were closed; the mission hospitals and clinics faced the blank choice of staying or going; farms were abandoned and black peasants put out of work. Recruitment to Zanu reached an all-time high. More than a thousand men a month were now leaving for Mozambique.

'Independence,' said Mugabe, 'is not negotiable.'

It was in this uncompromising mood that the Central Committee gathered in Chimoio in northern Mozambique on 31 August 1977 for a nine-day meeting that was finally to seal Mugabe's leadership. Under the open skies in the Chimoio refugee and guerrilla camp, Mugabe was proclaimed President of Zanu, both party and army.

'It was clear,' said Edgar Tekere three years later, 'clear to all of us, on the Central Committee, on the high command, on the general staff, and in the army, that at long last we had the man to lead us.'

Mugabe's call was for dedication, efficiency and effectiveness, both in the army and the party. He denounced the latest attempts at a settlement, the Anglo-American initiatives of Britain's foreign secretary, Dr David Owen, and America's UN ambassador, Andrew Young.

'They are just imperialist manoeuvres aimed at the neutralisation of our war effort and negating our successes and are being advanced through the instrumentality of a home-based stooge and reactionary leadership which, while in theory it pays lip service to the principle of majority rule, is in practice pandering to the bidding of its imperialist and settler masters to the detriment of the people's struggle.'

It wasn't just rhetoric. Mugabe had no faith at all in the Owen–Young moves. Publicly, in Dar-es-Salaam and Lusaka, he was forced to show at least willingness because of pressure from the Front Line. He recognised at once that Owen's brash, aggressive style of negotiating was bound to unite the Patriotic Front and the Front Line into resistance. To Young he was more well-disposed, but he never believed the appointment of one man by President Carter signalled wholesale changes in American policy. Owen and Young would still not exact the right concessions from Salisbury and Pretoria, of that he was convinced.

Nevertheless, he did appreciate that the two of them

were determined to bring the Patriotic Front into any settlement, far more so than Kissinger had been. Accordingly, Nkomo and Mugabe had been trying to build their fractious alliance throughout 1977. They met regularly, either in Maputo or Lusaka. As always, Mugabe pushed Nkomo for a greater commitment to the war, stressing the need for personal ambition to be sacrificed for the cause. Nkomo would insist that negotiations could still lead to a settlement: Mugabe argued for the 'armed struggle' as the only solution. Emnity was still strong, Nkomo positively loathed his trips to Maputo, 'enemy territory' as he called it. For months, their political union stalled short of becoming a military pact.

Whatever chances there were of forging closer ties were wrecked by the meeting of Ian Smith and Kenneth Kaunda in late September in Lusaka. There was no doubt that Smith was prepared to countenance an agreement with Nkomo through Kaunda, who had always seen Nkomo as the most likely and suitable to succeed to the presidency.

When the news of the secret meeting came out, Mugabe was furious. The meeting, he said, could only have been designed to promote Nkomo's chances of returning home and making a deal with Smith. Within his party, there was anger at Kaunda's part. Memories of the arrests after Chitepo's murder were still fresh.

Mugabe denounced Kaunda for meeting Smith and further demanded to know if Nkomo had been present. Kaunda said he hadn't. Mugabe said he did not believe that. Now, said Mugabe, he knew why Nkomo would not put all his forces into the war: he was waiting on a settlement with Smith, even perhaps for Smith to fall under pressure from South Africa and the West.

When the latest envoy of peace, Field Marshal Lord Carver, arrived in Dar-es-Salaam at the end of October, Nkomo and Mugabe did manage to go as the Patriotic Front. A two-day meeting had been planned, instead it lasted for just 70 minutes. Together they rejected out of hand the Anglo-American idea of a UN peacekeeping force to ensure a ceasefire, they wanted their own forces to police it. Furthermore, said Mugabe, there was no point in simply declaring a ceasefire: there must be precise plans for the hand-over of power as well.

Smith showed as little enthusiasm as Nkomo and Mugabe. He was already looking to an 'internal settlement' with the nationalists at home, Sithole and Muzorewa. First of all, he had to contain, if not crush, Mugabe's growing army and the threat it posed all along the border with Mozambique because any 'internal settlement' without Nkomo would inevitably induce an offensive from Zapu along the western front with Zambia and Botswana.

In November, the Rhodesians struck deep into Mozambique on their biggest raid so far. It did not change the course of the war, as Walls and Smith had hoped. But it did give them the breathing space to pursue a settlement independent of Washington, London and Pretoria.

It was about 7.30 in the morning of 23 November when the Rhodesian squadrons reached Chimoio. There were jet bombers, fighter planes, helicopters carrying paratroopers from the Air Force base at Umtali about 60 miles away. They strafed the camp, then bombed it, finally the paratroopers were dropped to finish off whoever and whatever remained.

Anne Tekere, Edgar Tekere's wife, was found by Tongogara three days later hiding in a latrine pit, where she stayed out of sight from the units of the Rhodesian African rifles who stayed for 48 hours after the first attack. Her account of the raid is worth recording here not just for its gruesome testimony – but also for the deep-rooted hatred of the white government it engendered in her husband and some of his colleagues on the Zanu Central Committee.

'The attack began just as the children were gathering for morning assembly,' recalled Mrs Tekere, who was a teacher in the camp. 'We heard first one aircraft, but the sky was overcast and so we did not see the bombers until they came above our heads. We were trying to disperse when there were explosions all around us and on top of us. The children were told to run into the bush.

'From then on it was impossible to gather the children in one place. We were not trained in military operations and we did not know what to do. There were smaller planes as well as the jet bombers, and some of them dropped paratroopers. And there were helicopters which machine-gunned people as they ran away.

'We had a small security force of about 100 soldiers who fought back with machine-guns, but their ammunition ran out after a few minutes. The bombs seemed to be a kind of acid or inflammable. They burned the children and set fire to the bush.

'I knew I could not run very much. When I looked towards Chimoio town I saw paratroopers landing and I decided to run and hide in a pit latrine. The fluid came up to my waist. Worst of all were the worms that crawled around me, but I felt safe because the pit was not destroyed by the bombs.

'All the time I was in the pit I heard explosions and shooting and I was too frightened to come out. I was afraid that if they had dogs they might find where I was and when I heard voices I was too frightened to call out.

'Then I heard an engine, a long distance away, and later I recognised people speaking in Shona. I called out and they found me. They tried to haul me up with a rope, but I had hurt my arm getting into the pit and could not tie the rope around me. They broke the pit, removing the logs. I heard one of my pupils asked, "Is that you Mrs Tekere?"'

Mugabe, who had broke down and wept when he heard the news of the raid at Nyazonia the year before, was enraged by this attack. Ranting at British diplomats in Maputo, he demanded to know how Britain could sit by and watch the 'slaughter of innocent refugees, women and children.'

He was further incensed by comments made by Dr Owen – and quoted by the BBC, which Mugabe listened to every day at his Maputo. The raids, said Owen, showed just how determined the Rhodesians were. 'How can I be expected to negotiate with that man (Owen) when he talks like that?' Mugabe said.

Whatever the facts about the number of guerrillas in the camp – the Rhodesians claimed they killed 1200 of them in the raid – the attack on Chimoio made any compromise from Mugabe impossible. It also prompted the final attempt by 'dissidents' to overthrow him.

For some time leading members of the Central Committee had questioned Mugabe's leadership on ideological and military grounds. They now tried to feed on the disarray and discontent created by the Chimoio raid to stage a coup against both Mugabe and Tongogara.

They were led by Rugare Gumbo, information secretary, and Henry Hamadziripi, manpower secretary. They were supported by several capable Zanla commanders in the camps. In trying to gain support, they made Mugabe's leadership and the direction he was taking the main issue. He was attacked for lack of military knowledge, for reluctance to go into the field with the guerrillas, and for even allowing himself to be seen to negotiate with the likes of Owen and Young. Mugabe and the high command were blamed for the Chimoio debacle. According to the rebels, the Chimoio camp was pitifully short of any defence system. (Privately, even the governments of Tanzania and Mozambique were appalled at the lack of security.)

Above all, they accused the leadership of failing to foster seriously the 'Marxism-Leninism-Mao Tse Tung thought' as laid down by the Chimoio Central Committee meeting the previous September. They wanted, just as Machingura had a year before, greater political power for the guerrillas themselves.

Mugabe initially thought the revolt could be solved by argument. When, however, in January he heard that its leaders had made contact with Nkomo in an attempt to gain power by combining Zanu with Zapu, he moved quickly. They were arrested just in time. They already had plans to kidnap Tongogara.

The rebellion was a bitter disappointment to Mugabe, who knew it might weaken his hand in dealing with Nkomo and the West. It saddened him because he knew that it could divide the party and the army. Even when Gumbo, Hamadziripi and former field commanders like Joseph Chimurenga were in jail, he refused to sanction the calls for executions made by some on his Central Committee.

Instead, he opted for a thorough 'clean-up' of the entire party. Not so much a purge, more a return to the principles of frugality and abstinence that Mugabe himself lived by. One of the charges against Gumbo had been that he had squandered party funds, travelling widely and living far too well throughout Africa and Europe. A party official in London was soon under investigation for buying a house there with party money. In Maputo, there were orders from Mugabe himself to all party members to watch their behaviour in public. President Machel had personally told him to put an immediate stop to the heavy drinking and the womanising that some senior Zanu men indulged in at the capital's few nightspots, like the Polana hotel.

At the end of January 1978 Mugabe, his house-cleaning well underway, left for talks in Malta with Nkomo, Young and Owen. Smith had already opened talks with Muzorewa and Sithole on an internal settlement. All the indications were that they would succeed and a transitional government would quickly follow.

Washington and Whitehall now wanted to prepare the

ground for negotiations between that government and the Patriotic Front. Malta helped. The PF accepted that the UN peacekeepers could have a role: but Mugabe still insisted that the guerrilla leaders had to control security during the transition.

'The trouble with Robert Mugabe,' said Young afterwards, 'is that when you've got a Jesuit education mixed with a Marxist ideology you've got a hell of a guy to deal with.' Nevertheless, despite his public obduracy, Mugabe was moving slowly towards a compromise on the basis of the Anglo-American plans.

Both he and Nkomo were worried that Britain might yet recognise an internal settlement. If the 'puppets Muzorewa and Sithole', as they liked to call them, were recognised then sanctions could be lifted and that might swing the war decisively in Salisbury's favour at the very time their guerrilla armies could take control.

By March, and a meeting of the PF in Tanzania, President Nyerere was forecasting quick agreement on the Anglo-American package. President Carter announced a fresh plan for an all-party conference, the momentum was growing for a settlement including the PF.

Carter's secretary of state, Cyrus Vance, Owen and Young got concessions but a rude shock when they met Mugabe and Nkomo in Dar-es-Salaam in April.

There were important agreements on the role of the president commissioner who would oversee the transition period; on the part to be played by the UN force; even that the Patriotic Front would not insist on controlling the governing council.

But Mugabe held out absolutely for his forces having 'the dominant role' in the security forces during the transition; and he stuck firmly to his demand that the only negotiating parties would be the Patriotic Front and the British.

Despite all that, Mugabe said yes, they were prepared to attend a conference.

As one of Owen's aides concluded: 'There's no point in going to a conference unless we have agreement on the substantive issues he's talking about.'

Smith's gamble on an internal settlement was based on one important belief, shared by him and Peter Walls: that Muzorewa and Sithole would be able to talk the guerrillas out of the bush and into peace. By the middle of 1978, with their settlement three months old, it was patently clear that they had misjudged the influence the two Nationalists had.

Just dozens, not hundreds, of guerrillas had taken advantage of an amnesty. Now Muzorewa and Sithole set about building their own armies.

Zanu's strength in the field now stood at about 8000 men, Zapu had infiltrated about a quarter of that number into the western front. It meant that the white farming communities were now in the front line, isolated and often surrounded: they were ambushed, kidnapped, blown up by landmines. The reasons for staying on diminished rapidly as the guerrillas stole their cattle, wrecked the cattle-dips which prevented disease among the herds, and forced an increasing number of their African labourers to desert. For settler communities now going into their third generation, 1978 was the beginning of the end. In the beautiful Penhalonga valley, north of Umtali and just across the border from Mozambique, just a handful of families stayed where there had once been over a hundred. Those who did now formed beleaguered pockets of white resistance. Mugabe's war meant they didn't go out at night, they travelled for supplies in heavily guarded convoys, their wives even worried about answering the phone for fear of telling guerrilla spies that they were on the farm. Ian Smith liked to talk about the inventive spirit of the Rhodesians. They now turned to making a bizarre assortment of mine-protected vehicles, often converting landrovers into mini-armouries with automatic machine-gun emplacements on the roof and side panels capable of firing dozens of rounds a minute.

The protected villages, where the Smith Government had forcibly housed tens of thousands of tribespeople to prevent 'subversion' by the guerrillas and stop them giving help to Mugabe's men, were no longer deemed necessary by the government in the eastern highlands and the south-east. The men who guarded them were needed to hold off the guerrilla advance towards towns in the area.

The government wouldn't admit but there was little point in having protected villages when the guerrillas already controlled most of the surrounding countryside.

Guerrilla claims to control of up to 70 per cent of the country were patently false. There were, in fact, few areas that the security forces could not go into once they had mustered their customary superiority in firepower.

But the tide of the war had turned. The guerrillas, for the first time, were winning. It was, as Mugabe would tell journalists visiting Maputo, only a matter of time. It might be one year, possibly five, but the result would be the same.

From May till October Mugabe was to launch an international offensive, travelling thousands of miles in search of moral and material support. He visited Moscow (where his poor relations with the Russians in Mozambique precluded him seeing any one of great importance), Vietnam, North Korea and Cuba. The Chinese were having their own problems at home after the death of Mao and the arrest of the gang of four. Supplies of arms and ammunition from Peking were running low. Through patient negotiations Mugabe was winning help from the Eastern bloc, never from Russia directly, but through Romania, Yugoslavia and Iraq. When he met Castro for the second time in a few weeks, at Ethiopia's revolution day celebrations in September, they formally sealed long-term plans for Cuban advisers to train Mugabe's men in camps in Mozambique, Angola and Ethiopia. That rang alarm bells in Washington and London, increasing the pressure on David Owen to rescue the Anglo-American plans from the ruins of the negotiations in previous months.

But Owen was now seriously hampered by the growing feeling in the West that there should be no compromise with Mugabe and his 'bloodthirsty guerrilla war'.

One incident, in June, had done the cause of detente with the Patriotic Front more damage than anything before it.

On 23 June, a gang attacked the Elim Mission station in the Vumba mountains on the Mozambique border, one of the few that had stayed open in the face of the war.

Eight British missionaries and four children – one of them just a month old – were massacred. A ninth died later in hospital.

Missions had been attacked before but the savagery of this particular incident drew world-wide condemnation. The women victims were raped. When the security forces arrived they found one lady bludgeoned and bayonetted to death with her arm reaching out towards her baby murdered beside her. Another child, in her pyjamas, carried the imprints of a boot on her shattered head.

In Britain, crowded congregations at Elim Pentecostal churches prayed for forgiveness for those responsible. But elsewhere, notably the British parliament, there were calls for the immediate cessation of any talks with Mugabe – and the immediate recognition of the internal settlement.

The evidence pointed unmistakably to Mugabe's forces being responsible. Within weeks, he countered the charge. The Selous Scouts, the crack unit of the Rhodesian army, were responsible, he said, in an attempt to provoke a world-wide backlash against the guerrillas' cause.

'What do we stand to gain by killing missionaries?' he asked in an interview in Maputo. 'What do we ever stand to gain? Does that promote our military progress in any way? Aren't we capable of establishing, by virtue of purely logical reasons, that an act of this nature would be a setback to our revolution? Let no one doubt us when we say we did not commit this act of brutality.'

Mugabe meant what he said, remarked one Western diplomat on hearing that. 'But for his own self-protection he had better come to terms with the fact that some of his men would prefer racial slaughter.'

Certainly the rhetoric coming out of Maputo seemed to suggest just that. In August, Mugabe was quoted by his own party magazine *Zimbabwe News* as saying that Muzorewa, Sithole and Chief Jeremiah Chirau would be killed for their 'crime' of signing the internal settlement with Smith back in March. An editorial added: 'No one Zimbabwean – be he cleric or chief or humble citizen – should be allowed to prey upon the people in this way. The wages of sin are well known. The people's hand is long, their memories are wrought with blood and their punishment is certain.

'So it is written, so let it be done.'

It was *Zimbabwe News* that carried a death sentence for Ian Smith as well.

Mugabe was asked: 'Would you try Mr Smith and other principals for war crimes?'

He replied: 'Mr Smith is a criminal, he has committed all kinds of very serious crimes. The massacres he has committed here upon Zimbabwean refugees in Mozambique, in Zambia, in Botswana, all these put together warrant very stern judgement by the people. They call for the death penalty in my opinion, but again I am not the person to pronounce it.

'I can only judge that this type of evidence merits the

111

passing of capital punishment, but we will have him tried by the people – if by the time we take over he will still be around.'

Smith, it seemed, had every intention of being around for some time to come. The internal settlement had got him nowhere. To end the war, he had to have recognition from Britain and America. He might get it if he could persuade Nkomo to join it. Smith's summer offensive was on the diplomatic front. Kenneth Kaunda encouraged it, the British helped.

Smith and Nkomo met in Lusaka with absolute secrecy in the middle of August. Neither of them had said a word about it to their respective 'partners', Muzorewa and Sithole on Smith's side, Mugabe on Nkomo's.

Nkomo was, to say the least, attracted by Smith's offer to make him effectively head of government until elections were held. Nkomo, out of self-protection more than anything else, wanted Mugabe included in the settlement. If not he would have a war on his hands too.

They agreed to meet a few days later and invite Mugabe. What followed was arguably the most bizarre highlight of years of distrust, suspicion and emnity not only between Nkomo and Mugabe but among the nationalists in general. Nkomo simply could not bring himself to tell ('confess' might be more appropriate) Mugabe that he had been negotiating with Smith without him. It was left to the Nigerians, who had actively encouraged the talks. They called Mugabe to Lagos and gave him the news. He was enraged and refused on the spot to see Smith. So, too, were Nyerere and Machel when they found out about Kaunda's involvement.

Mugabe and Nkomo met in Lusaka at the beginning of September. Nkomo's version – that Smith seemed ready to surrender, so he had talked to him – did little to palliate Mugabe who was reported to have told Nkomo: 'You would just be another of Smith's puppets.'

Two days later, the deal was off. It wasn't because of Mugabe's resistance.

Nkomo's men shot down a Viscount airliner near Kariba and massacred most of the survivors. There was no way that Smith's white constituency would countenance any negotiation with Nkomo.

Within weeks the Rhodesian Air Force was conducting bombing raids into Zambia with impunity. And the Patriotic Front was united now more than ever.

'Unless Nkomo joins the internal settlement,' said Mugabe, 'we are confident that the Patriotic Front will stick together. In the past few years we have managed, against considerable odds, to keep Nkomo on the right side. We have learned how to work with him and with Zapu. In addition, there is the pressure from other African States and, of course, from the Zimbabwean people themselves.

'No, I am certain there will be no war between the two components of the Patriotic Front.'

There was still the war against the Salisbury Government, however. And at the end of 1978 Mugabe christened the new year 'The Year of the People's Storm'.

However much Mugabe may have disliked the rhetoric of slogans and hyperbole – and he did – he recognised their propaganda value. And he used them when necessary.

'The final blow, the most decisive knock-out by the people's mailed fist, must be effected soon,' he wrote to the Zanla cadres in the field. 'The enemy is battered and dazed. Let us now move towards him with all our mustered reserves, remembering always that ours is a people's war, fought by the people and for the people.

'Victory assuredly awaits us and cannot elude us. Never!' Others had seen another Mugabe, the leader shorn of the dogma and need to bolster morale in the field. A man, it seemed, of that African rarity, of both intellect and principle. One such 'viewing' of Mugabe was

113

in the northern Italian city of Reggio Emilia in November 1978. Italy's multitude of political parties had organised a 'Southern Africa solidarity conference'.

This was Mugabe at his best, displaying the quality of his self-education, his understanding of world politics and his belief in the ethics of his cause.

Above all, he showed just how adept he was at tailoring his vocabulary, presentation and theme to suit his audience. He was mastering the arts of political life which were to serve him so well as Lancaster House and after independence. Here, for the first time, he was to reveal them in the West.

To evident Italian amazement, he began with a mini discourse on Italian history – its transformation from empire to democratic republic, through Mazzini and Machiavelli to Mussolini and then to the present-day Italy.

Southern Africa was going through something similar and it needed help from those who had already reached democracy. 'Our fighting front will forever need your reinforcing rear,' he said.

He then took his audience through the history of the past year of negotiations: the impasse at Malta; the PF acceptance of cardinal issues at Dar-es-Salaam; Smith's secret talks with Nkomo; and abandonment by both Washington and London, of the Anglo-American proposals. Through the power of his argument, and the fine weaving of his thesis, Mugabe led his audience to his conclusion. 'Our belief remains that armed struggle is, in our circumstances, the only effective instrument for achieving our goal of national independence and thus creating peace in our country.'

It was the kind of verbal mastery that the Italians love, especially their politicians. It won him a standing ovation. 'Whatever you may think about his politics and his war,' said one cabinet minister from Italy's ruling Christian Democrat party, 'he convinces you because he seems to see almost all the sides to the argument – and still believes he is right.'

At the end of the year Sally Mugabe wrote to Lady Walston. She had been in London in the autumn, visiting a younger brother of Mugabe's who was dying in hospital. But she had missed seeing the Walstons. Now she brought them up to date. 'Regarding our struggle, we are still at it you know. This year we congratulate ourselves for many achievements but we continue to be cautious and guard against complacency, for the enemy has now been driven to desperation,' she wrote.

'All the fighting is at home in Zimbabwe but the enemy continues to attack our rear base countries, inflicting untold sufferings upon the people of Mozambique and Zambia. The reason is quite simple, to force these countries to stop supporting the just struggle for freedom. Fortunately, we have good friends who will always stand by us.

'Above all, we ourselves have the will to free our country.... Sure, victory will be ours.'

Early in the new year Mugabe warned his Central Committee that they should expect major diplomatic and military offensives from the Western powers and Salisbury in the year ahead.

He knew that Peter Walls would be under strict orders to produce the best possible climate for the 'internal settlement' elections in April. Whatever chances the settlement had of winning international acceptance depended largely on a high turn-out being complemented by a down-turn in the war. That might persuade the West to call the Salisbury Government 'representative'. Mugabe's battle-plan was to step up the war, taking it closer to the cities than ever before, while making his army spread the message that the people must boycott the poll. This was the year of the People's Storm in the People's War. The guerrillas must be educated to understand that they were now not just fighting but also teaching, building a constituency for whenever the party might need it. It needed it now to prevent Smith, Muzorewa and Sithole winning enough African support for their settlement.

In December, the guerrillas had pulled off their most audacious and embarrassing attack of the war to date, bombing the biggest fuel depot in the heart of Salisbury and starting a five-day fire that consumed nearly a month's fuel supplies. Now Tongogara issued the most detailed orders for attacks on the capital. In January, hundreds of men were moved into the tribal trustlands closest to Salisbury.

Mugabe realised that, if the election was even moderately successful, he would come under pressure immediately from Britain and America to make his peace with the new leaders in Salisbury. To resist that, he needed his independence more than ever. And he needed new friends. In the first few weeks of the year, he was to assiduously nurture contacts with the Ethiopians, the Cubans and his allies in the Eastern bloc (Romania, Yugoslavia). Even the East Germans, hitherto faithful to the Kremlin's policy of downgrading Mugabe, came to Maputo in March. Mugabe did not see them, he carefully left it to Simon Muzenda. The Chinese invasion of Vietnam was on their minds and before talking aid and arms, they asked Muzenda to issue a statement with them condemning Peking.

Muzenda, for all his kind, avuncular charm, has a temper. He told them he was extremely insulted by the suggestion. If Zanu wanted to issue any such statement – and it didn't – it certainly would not require help from the East Germans or anyone else. The 'contract' between East Germany and Zanu was over before it had even begun.

Whatever the heated exchanges, though, Mugabe's diplomatic sorties had two very important effects on the West. By moving, albeit very slowly, towards the Soviet satellite states (Ethiopia, Cuba) he was demonstrating his readiness for a long drawn-out guerrilla war if necessary. And such a war would surely prevent the West from either recognising the Smith–Muzorewa deal *or* trying once more to talk Nkomo into the settlement.

Still, the chances of Nkomo joining it did worry Mugabe, President Nyerere even more so. Mugabe's tactic was to remind Nkomo constantly of his duty to the Patriotic Front and to the stark choice he faced. It was something akin to psychological warfare between the two, Mugabe making Nkomo feel that he had to choose one way or the other while warning of the dire consequences if he went the wrong way. 'If the people are not prepared to fight in the struggle,' Mugabe said, 'then they must not expect to find themselves at the helm of government which is the result of the victories of the people.'

Compared to what had been feared, the elections were a qualified success. Walls put on a massive show of firepower throughout the country in the final week of the campaign, and, although there were clashes in the trustlands near Salisbury, the guerrillas quickly opted to lie low when they saw the enemy's numbers and armoury.

The turn-out was better than expected. In the cities it was high, in the rural areas the guerrillas clearly were able to keep the voters away. Muzorewa's victory was by no means meaningless, as several independent observers noted: but the election overall still fell some way short of persuading Britain and America to recognise the government. Or did it? On 3 May Margaret Thatcher was elected by a large majority, returning the Conservatives to power for the first time since October 1974, the days when Mugabe was still in detention and men like Sithole were recognised nationalist leaders.

Loyd Boyd, a former Conservative colonial secretary, had been sent by Mrs Thatcher to observe the election. His verdict was that it had been as 'free and fair' as possible. Sally Mugabe was in Sweden for several weeks after the election giving talks throughout the country to infants, high-school pupils and university undergraduates. When she returned to Maputo, she found Mugabe seriously concerned about the approach of the Thatcher Government. She shared them, as she told Lady Walston.

'The political situation in Zimbabwe is unstable as usual,' she wrote. 'But this time it seems lady Thatcher's government are bent on doing something out of the ordinary, by lifting sanctions and recognising an illegal regime.

'It would create a very sad state of affairs, if, for the sake of 180,000 whites, Britain were to compromise her principles. Should this happen, the question would be: why did Britain not recognise Smith's government in 1965 ... if Smith committed no illegality?

'And why all this suffering on millions of people – sanctions, executions, decades of imprisonment, broken marriages, orphans, widows etc etc?

'What does Lady Thatcher want to prove, that she is a racist? I suspect she is ... it would only be a racist who would underscore the Smith–Muzorewa regime.'

But Mrs Thatcher was to surprise everyone at the Commonwealth conference in Lusaka at the beginning of August.

On the face of it, the summit in Zambia was just like any one of the dozens of attempts made over the years to get an agreement on Rhodesia. There were the same circumstances working for peace – the desperate need of the Front Line States for a peace that would enable them to put their shattered economies back together again, and the personal wishes of men like Kaunda and Nyerere to avoid having an international conflict in Southern Africa.

And there were much the same objections as always – primarily that Mugabe and Nkomo could not be expected to accept anything less than equality with the nationalists, be it on a military or a political level, in any transition leading to fresh elections.

Not even Mrs Thatcher thought she would succeed in getting an agreement for an all-party conference at the Lusaka summit. Mugabe certainly didn't. He sent Edgar Tekere as an observer-cum-lobbyist and his secretary-general arrived in town with a statement positively bristling with animosity towards the new British prime minister.

'Mrs Thatcher will be fighting to have the conference totally ignore the vitally important question of the need to get rid of the evil settler racist armed forces and have them replaced by the people's patriotic force.

'She will fight hard to ignore this vital question because her racist mind deeply appreciates that the minority racist settler interest will remain securely entrenched by the racist settler forces on whose back treacherous Muzorewa rides.'

It may have sounded to Mrs Thatcher like something out of a Marxist primer, but she was not to be deterred. She arrived exuding phrases like, 'I will not be bullied, you know.'

She knew her greatest element would be surprise, and she played to it. When she made her opening address to the conference virtually every delegation would have predicted bitter disagreement by the end of it.

Instead, they heard what they thought was an olive branch. It quickly turned into what they could only interpret as wholesale compromises from the British.

The British prime minister was saying that her government was prepared to decolonise Rhodesia and bring it to independence just like they had Kenya and Tankanyika. She knew Britain's responsibilities and she was determined to fulfil them. Furthermore, she was saying the internal settlement was 'defective' because its constitution gave the whites power disproportionate to their size in the community. Her ideal would be a more balanced one, where the whites would have an entrenched position in parliament but it would be genuine black majority rule.

Perhaps because men like Nyerere and Kaunda had expected so little, they reacted so much. Whatever the precise chemistry was, they were delighted.

Immediately a 'contact' group of six – Tanzania, Zambia, Nigeria, Jamaica, Australia – sat down with Mrs Thatcher and Lord Carrington, her foreign secretary to hammer out the details. Layer by layer, step by step, they built a working agreement for an all-party conference to consider. Some wanted a peacekeeping force but that had ominous memories of the Anglo-American plans. The transition and elections 'under British government authority with Commonwealth observers' cleared that long-standing obstacle. After years of bitterness, suspicion and distrust, there was agreement within a few hours. No one exactly danced in the streets, but Mrs Thatcher did manage a waltz with Kenneth Kaunda.

No one yet knew whether Mugabe and Nkomo would attend the conference, called for London in September. But the agreement of the Front Line States made it a request they couldn't refuse.

For once, Nkomo seemed a trifle lost for words. 'An all-party conference?' he asked. 'What are all the parties? We (the PF) are the only factor in the situation.'

When word came from Maputo, it was Mugabe demanding that the Rhodesian security forces be disbanded and replaced by the guerrillas. That was just one pre-condition for elections. Mugabe wouldn't say it, but he was already negotiating.

Chapter 5 — Lancaster House

It must have been an incongruous sight. The opening day of the Lancaster House conference. The formalities over, 60-odd delegates retire to a reception in one of those magnificent, huge gallery rooms overlooking St James's Park. In one corner Ian Smith, sticking closely to members of his own delegation, spies Josiah Tongogara in another. Mugabe's General and Mugabe's enemy number one nod at each other. They had last met in Geneva four years before, but their ties went back a lot further – to Tongogara's childhood in Selukwe, Smith's home town south of Salisbury. As a child 'Tongo' had helped on the Smith homestead. Come harvest time he, along with the rest of his family, would work on the Smith farm. It was 25 years since Tongogara had been there but he remembered Grandma Smith, Ian Smith's mother.

Tongogara's massive frame belied a ruthless general. It also concealed his extraordinary gentleness with those he liked. He made the first move.

'How is the old lady?' he asked Smith.

'Very well, thank you, although she's much older now,' Smith replied.

Tongogara smiled.

'Please send her my warm wishes,' he said. 'I've often thought of the old lady. She used to give me sweets, you know.'

Smith would never talk about that conversation. Tongogara liked to and weeks later – when the conference was set to collapse, with the Smith–Muzorewa Government going home to probable recognition from Britain and war from Tongogara's men – he was to recall it as the moment when he realised for the first time there could be a negotiated peace.

'In itself the few words we exchanged weren't important. What was important was the realisation for me that the war was not about personalities, it wasn't Mugabe and Tongogara versus Smith and Walls, it wasn't about Black versus White, but the system, the system of oppression...

'I didn't want to destroy Smith or the old lady. I did want to destroy the system he had built.'

The Mugabes had arrived in London on 7 September. British Special Branch had specially chosen the Royal Garden Hotel in Kensington High Street for the 40-strong Zanu delegation. It's a modern, high-rise block relatively easy to secure and they were genuinely worried about Mugabe's safety, more than any other delegate to the conference. At once security became an issue. Memories of that hotel fire in Geneva were long. Mugabe was uncomfortable enough already in an expensive hotel which his frugality didn't need. He wanted his own bodyguards. The British insisted on Special Branch being there as well. They won, and Mugabe was to spend the next fifteen weeks surrounded day and night by two members of Special Branch and two of his own Zanu 'Protocol' unit. The closest the four of them got was in a discussion over respective hand weapons.

Nkomo, Muzorewa, even Smith had some to the conference quietly optimistic of a settlement. Mugabe was anything but. More than anyone, he had always believed in the 'Armed Struggle' almost as an end in itself to prepare his party for power. By the time he arrived, he was not only sceptical but also cynical about the chances of an agreement. If he had to return to war, it would be no great loss. He was deeply suspicious of Mrs Thatcher and the Conservatives. He believed, to a large extent, that Lancaster House would simply enable the Tories to justify recognition of the Muzorewa–Smith Government and so palliate the right-wing of the Conservative Party, 'The Julian Amerys of this world,' as he called them.

Caught very briefly in the lobby of the Royal Garden on the weekend before the conference opened, he was an apparent model of intransigence.

'We have not come here to negotiate with Smith, or Muzorewa. We have not come here to negotiate the principle of majority rule. We have come here to negotiate with the British the transfer of power. Nothing else is for discussion.'

It sounded like a replay of Geneva. Except that this time Mugabe was determined not to make the same mistakes. For a start, he wasn't going to lose the propaganda battle. Mugabe knew from Geneva that there would be as much negotiation in public – on television, in the papers – as in the conference room. Accordingly, this time Zanu was going to negotiate with the help, if not through, the media. For that purpose Mugabe himself had chosen Eddison Zvobgo, an American-educated lawyer who had become de facto Information Secretary in Zanu after the purge of Gumbo two years earlier. Zvobgo liked to boast that he'd been the master of ceremonies at the very first Zanu press conference, in Salisbury in 1963, that he had friends ranging from Ethiopia's Colonel Mnegistu to Teddy Kennedy, and that, above all, he had Mugabe's ear. In the weeks to come he was to grab headlines quite literally. His flair for producing the quick and easy quote for pressmen, and performing for the television cameras was very conscious. It culminated in one bizarre evening just 10 days before peace was signed, when he was to tell Mrs Thatcher to 'jump in the Thames' and suggest that she was 'in concubinage with Satan Botha' (the South African prime minister).

The tone and nature of both his argument and language led the Foreign Office to denounce him in private as the wild man of the conference – 'he likes a drink a little too much,' was how one Foreign Office man put it – and that he didn't even represent the views of Mugabe and his Central Committee.

Nothing could have been further from the truth. Zvobgo was a very conscious 'plant' by Mugabe. He was worried about Nkomo's performances in public, he knew only too well how his partner in the Patriotic Front could put his foot in it. Zvobgo, as a constitutional lawyer, was made the senior Front spokesman to avoid that. He would handle the media, usually for both of them. Furthermore, Zvobgo was under strict orders to push the hard line. While Mugabe might be making concessions in conference, Zvobgo would be fighting for and defending the Armed Struggle in the eyes of the world.

The only other pessimist on Day One was Peter Carrington. When Mrs Thatcher won the election in May, the Foreign Secretary quite clearly had options other than this quest for an all-party settlement. The tide in the Conservative Party, as Mugabe knew well, was running unmistakably in favour of a deal with Bishop Muzorewa – recognition for his government, the lifting of sanctions, and the chance for General Walls to do what he'd always preached. Smash the Patriotic Front. It would have been condemned by every government in Africa apart from Pretoria, decried at the United nations, hammered by the Commonwealth. But it would have palliated the right-wing of the Conservative Party, Mrs Thatcher's own power base after all. And the right argued: 'Do it now and weather the storm. Put it off and you'll never get the likes of Mugabe to the negotiating table anyway.'

That Lord Carrington didn't take that low road – as it undoubtedly would have been – says everything about the man and his particular brand of politics. There have been those even among his supporters who have thought of him as 'the gentleman amateur'. The label devalues the quality of his intellect and the strength of his purpose.

124

Carrington, in his early days in politics, was a disciple of Harold Macmillan. As such, his first primer on Africa was the 'wind of change' speech. Macmillan's high Tory line in that had been Britain's responsibility to its colonies in Africa. Historically, Macmillan said, we educated and lifted the people of Africa, we supplied everything from missionaries to armies, teachers to traders. Now it was Britain's duty to lead them to independence responsibly. His warning was that failure to fulfil that responisbility would see the West outflanked by Moscow in the continent.

It was this philosophy that had now brought Carrington to the high road on Rhodesia – high-risk maybe but the only route for a politician with his strong principles.

Ethics apart, however, Carrington had got lucky, as one of his aides joked after Lusaka. The Commonwealth summit – and that remarkable meeting of the Front Line States – had shown a genuine appetite for peace. Nyerere of Tanzania couldn't afford the war much longer, Kaunda of Zambia might not survive if it went on, Machel of Mozambique had realised it was a threat to his young revolution. Individually none of them was likely to persuade Mugabe and Nkomo into peace, collectively they gave Carrington a strong lever on them both to pursue a settlement. Not at any price, but certainly on terms that would have been unthinkable even a few months before.

Carrington's Foreign Office liked to talk in euphemisms. Rhodesia, they said, was 'ripe for the picking'. Carrington himself had another phrase. He wanted to 'lance the boil' once and for all. Still, in the days just before Lancaster House, the Foreign Secretary was pessimistic. He really didn't believe, when it came to it, that he would succeed where so many others had failed. He knew he could have an agreement with Muzorewa, the low road, the 'second-class solution' as the press called it. He sensed that he could bring Nkomo in too.

But Mugabe? Time and again in the weeks to come Carrington would be asked that one. And time and again he would come with the answer that no politician likes to give: 'I don't know.'

Mugabe, even by his own admittance, made a slow start to the conference. He was at best 'quiet' (his own estimate), at times 'downright bullish' (the Foreign Office), to his enemies 'disinterested because he's going to walk out anyway' (Muzorewa). He realised from day one that this was going to be a long conference – unless he did walk out. By the end of September, with the conference still haggling over procedure, he and Sally moved to an apartment in Bayswater. Some delegates, like Ian Smith, took a delight in sightseeing and taking in a football match every weekend. The Mugabes had time only for the conference and the long Central Committee meetings that followed almost every session at Lancaster House. Their huge flat was always crowded, up to 20 people staying at times. Sally had brought a handful of Zanu office girls from Maputo. From the way she organised the shopping, the laundry and meals, it was clear the Mugabes were digging in for a long stay in London.

As his performance in conference betrayed, Mugabe was unhappy. The rows with Smith and Muzorewa through the chair over who controlled what in Rhodesia and who had a right to be at Lancaster House were routine rhetoric. What worried him was the stance of the British. He already recognised a policy of attrition in Carrington, designed to wear him down into concessions. Occasionally, Mugabe lost his temper with 'the good Lord' as he called him with his best strain for the sardonic – and suspicion.

'We will not be bullied, Mr Chairman,' he would tell Carrington in a voice trembling with anger and frustration. 'We have not fought the war to give it all away in

Sally driving home her own message – Zimbabwe Grounds, 27 January 1980. *(Neil Libbert)*

'The biggest crowd Rhodesia has ever seen' – a white policeman's verdict on the homecoming rally. *(Neil Libbert)*

A face in the crowd – Zimbabwe Grounds, 27 January 1980. *(Neil Libbert)*

Muzenda, Mugabe and Edgar Tekere at the press conference after the attack on his home in Quorn Avenue, February 1980. *(Popperfoto)*

'Lord Soames must choose between war and peace' – Mugabe addresses an election rally at Fort Victoria, 10 February 1980, about an hour before an abortive assassination attempt. *(Popperfoto)*

Mugabe speaking at the Fort Victoria rally, the last of his campaign. *(Frank Herrmann, Sunday Times)*

A party worker covers the leader with the cockerel, symbol of ZANU (PF) as Mugabe chats to supporters in Salisbury, February 1980. *(Neil Libbert)*

Mugabe hears the news of the landslide at home in Quorn Avenue – 4 March 1980. *(Frank Herrmann, Sunday Times)*

'Let us join together' – Mugabe addresses the nation after the victory,
4 March 1980. *(Neil Libbert)*

The new First Lady of Zimbabwe – Sally at home on the day of the election result. *(Geoff Dalglish, Camera Press)*

The Mugabes at home in Quorn Avenue after the result is announced, 4 March 1980. *(Geoff Dalglish, Camera Press)*

'Old rivals, old enemies in one government' – Prime Minister Mugabe and Interior Minister Nkomo take up their seats in the new Zimbabwe Parliament, March 1980. *(Popperfoto)*

Mugabe, Lord Soames and Nkomo share a joke as the new Government is announced at Government House, March 1980. *(Popperfoto)*

Mugabe comes home to Kutama in triumph – 7 June 1980. *(Popperfoto)*

a matter of minutes.' Before long Mugabe had come to the conclusion that the Foreign Secretary was prepared to go ahead with the second-class solution. Indeed, he believed the bargain had been struck even before the conference started. But he was determined that, if the conference were to fail, international opinion would not condemn him for going back to war. Unlike Geneva, he would be seen this time to have exhausted all the possibilities for peace.

It was in this spirit that he and Nkomo agreed to the British Constitution on 18 October. 'It's no more than a way of letting the conference go forward,' Mugabe confided to a handful of reporters that night, 'it doesn't mean we like it.' It wasn't surprising Zanu didn't like it. It was hardly a blueprint for Socialism. The whites, even though they'd lost the de facto veto they had under the Smith–Muzorewa settlement, would be guaranteed 20 per cent of the seats in the new parliament. And on land the constitution protected property rights to a degree that made Zanu's long-time promise to redistribute the white farmlands to the people look hollow, if not downright false. Mugabe didn't say it but he was keeping his powder dry (if the Foreign Office liked farming and medical terms, Zanu always turned to guns) for the two issues that mattered most to him – the transitional period leading to elections and the ceasefire.

Nevertheless, Zvobgo fired a shot for him with the first of the warnings that were to haunt the conference from here on in. 'If Carrington carries on the way he has begun, plotting with the puppets (Muzorewa and Smith), we will go back to war. And have no doubts, Lord Carrington, there will be no peace.'

There were those at the Foreign Office who believed that up till now Nkomo and Mugabe had been stalling for time to get their men back across the borders from Zambia and Mozambique. The conference, they argued, would now push ahead. They failed to recognise the grave doubts in Mugabe's mind about any solution apart from war.

Peter Walls certainly didn't. The Commander-in-Chief of the Rhodesian Forces arrived in London in the third week of October. He was to sober the minds of everyone. If Ian Smith had confined himself to the occasional snipe at Mugabe across the conference table, General Walls was to stop little short of a fresh declaration of war.

Six months before, Walls had been admitting privately that Salisbury would be threatened within a year unless there was a settlement. Now he saw a deal with the British as the way to finish off the Patriotic Front before they finished him. On Saturday 27 October, after the toughest backstage bargaining of the whole conference, Bishop Muzorewa swallowed his fierce pride and agreed to dismantle his government, step down as prime minister and hand over power to a British governor. Carrington's game-plan – of getting Muzorewa and the whites to agree first, then turning to Mugabe and Nkomo with the second-class solution already achieved – was working. The pressure was on the Front to accept or be locked out. At Mugabe's apartment, some of his aides saw some comedy in it.

'Have you heard about the conversations between Carrington and Muzorewa?' one of them asked.

'Peter (Carrington) rings up Abel (Muzorewa) and says "Abel, will you?" – to which Muzorewa replies, "Before you go on, Peter, the answer's yes."'

Walls was anything but light-hearted about the agreement between Muzorewa and the British. Two days later he agreed to give his first interview to David Smith. Even for the man who'd once given his troops the simple edict 'the terrorists don't rest on Sundays, neither will we', and was apt to remark that any one of his men 'could see off a helluva lot of terrorists', it was a remarkable display of strength.

Smith: General, you have said for some time now that

the conflict requires a political solution. Do you still believe that's possible?

Walls: Yes, I think we are getting it. Surely what is happening now is exactly what people like myself have been suggesting should happen. I don't believe that you can have a political solution without having military strength and stability, without having economic stability and growth, resilience, but the point is that with the evolution that we have now, with our government's acceptance of the British proposals, I believe there is a way open for a fairly quick return to normality as far as the politics scene is concerned.

Smith: But with or without the Patriotic Front?

Walls: With or without the Patriotic Front, thank you, you have answered it. I don't care. But there is a chance for political stability. In fact if the British proposals go through there will be political stability. Sanctions will be lifted, we will be recognised not just by the British but by the rest of the world, I hope, by all fairminded people and I believe most of them have already indicated that they will accept us.

Smith: But if the Front doesn't come in, General, the war will go on.

Walls: That's right. And then the Front will be demolished.

Mugabe was incensed, Tongogara no less so. And worse still for Carrington, Walls had immeasurably deepened the Front's mistrust of Salisbury at the very moment when the Foreign Secretary was trying to persuade Mugabe and Nkomo that they must accept the machinery of the Salisbury Government as the only one capable of leading the country to elections. The British proposals for the transition leading to a poll were unequivocal: the governor would base his administration on the white-dominated civil service of Salisbury and he would keep law and order during the campaign through the existing Rhodesian police force. The supreme commander of that police force was Peter Walls.

'I believe the English have a phrase about smelling a rat.' said Zvobgo in one of his nightly press conferences, 'well, we smell a rat.'

On 1 November, two days after that interview, Mugabe went on the offensive inside the conference room for the first time. Britain, he said, was using the conference to bring about the capitulation of the Patriotic Front. The British plans were a plot to bring Muzorewa to power. The country would be led to elections by an administration biased towards Muzorewa.

Bring in the UN with a peacekeeping force, he insisted.

Carrington's 'No' was a one-word answer.

Mugabe's voice was now raised in genuine anger. 'If ever there was case for a UN peacekeeping force, this was it. But we will win without this conference, even though it may take time ... unless Lord Carrington relents, we will pack our bags and go back to war.'

Peter Walls, by all accounts, did not say a word.

In the next few days, Mugabe was to enlist the support of his friends in Africa. Carrington, he felt, had to be shocked out of the belief that the Front Line States did want peace at almost any price and would pressure him into ending the war, whatever the concessions.

First the Mozambicans.

'The ultimata, the blackmail and the constant suggestion from the British that this is the last chance for the Patriotic Front are arrogant attitudes,' said the government in Maputo. 'On many occasions, the representatives of Great Britain have tried to substitute the need for clear and constructive dialogue with threats, pressure and imposition ... they are organising the conditions for a civil war in Zimbabwe.'

Then Nyerere, from his home in Dar-es-Salaam.

'For the first time a rebellion has been ended not because the colonial power went in and fought the rebels but because the native people themselves took up arms and fought and conditions then became right for the colonial power to appoint a governor ... The British are appointing that governor because the Patriotic Front decided to fight Smith ... so really the Patriotic Front are allies of the British and really they ought to be treated that way ... and Walls ought to be sacked.'

On 7 November Mugabe and Sally took some rare time off to have Lord and Lady Walston to lunch. At last, Mugabe felt free to talk – and Lord Walston felt strongly enough about their meeting to write personally to Carrington the following day.

The point of principle made by Nyerere in Dar-es-Salaam was crucial, Lord Walston wrote.

'To understand Mugabe's approach, one has to recognise that his thinking and attitudes are based on the deep-rooted conviction that the British government is negotiating with what is still a rebel regime, and that any moves in the past few years towards a settlement have been brought only by the Patriotic Front's activities.

'In addition, Mugabe has a mistrust of Lord Carrington and some other political figures. We hope we may have had some influence in allaying these fears at least so far as the Foreign Secretary is concerned. However, we would urge some informal personal contacts.

'Apart from the fact that he undoubtedly wishes for a peaceful settlement, our main impression was that Mugabe had grave doubts about the openness of the British side in the negotiations. While he accepted that HMG was very anxious to achieve a settlement, he believes that they are strongly in favour of Muzorewa, and are working to ensure that he is head of the next Government.

'We gained the impression, that while he hoped the talks would succeed and the fighting would stop, he was not prepared for a peaceful solution except under the right conditions, and would continue the armed struggle

131

if he could not get satisfaction on the outstanding points.'

No doubt to emphasise just that, Mugabe flew to Ethiopia just two days after that lunch to see Colonel Mengistu and discuss the training of Zanla recruits, under Cuban instructors, at a camp just outside Addis Ababa. Meanwhile the Voice of Zimbabwe, the radio station President Machel had set up for Mugabe in Maputo for him to broadcast to his men in the bush, carried a personal message from him to the troops. He told them to ignore Lancaster House and step up operations inside Rhodesia. He ended by saying: 'Comrades, let us gain freedom from British colonial rule. A Lotta continua!'

Carrington was to remark that despite all the warnings, he'd heard no one suggest that Mugabe had walked out of the conference. Peace was still on. Just.

On 8 November Kenneth Kaunda, never a man to miss the international stage, flew to London. His worries were largely the same as Nyerere's and Machel's – that Nkomo and Mugabe would not be given a fair chance to negotiate a fair deal and so would abandon the conference.

But Kaunda had something else on his mind as well. He feared that Mugabe and Nkomo would split the Front, Mugabe heading for war, Nkomo partner to a peace that might not be worth the paper it was signed on. He'd come to urge unity and moderation, in that order.

Mugabe and many leading members of his Central Committee always suspected that Kaunda had been an architect of peace at Lusaka because he felt the time was right for Nkomo to return to Rhodesia and fight an election. And that Kaunda would have sanctioned an agreement that excluded Mugabe. Kaunda was, in fact, desperate for peace more because of the effects of the war on Zambia than any hopes he nurtured for Nkomo. And he was bitterly upset over the decision to split the PF for the election.

132

Mugabe and Nkomo had always been unhappy partners, it was a coalition of convenience rather than mutual respect or common goals. It wasn't just the tribal rivalry – Mugabe being Shona; Nkomo, Ndebele. Ideologically, they were worlds apart. Nkomo was a nationalist before he was a socialist, Mugabe a socialist before he was a nationalist. Mugabe disliked what he saw as Nkomo's expediency – arms from Moscow, financial support from the Lonrho mining Empire. He himself jealously protected his independence ('China is a friend but no more than that') and had always insisted that there would be no strings attached to any help he got. Above all, there was the deep mistrust of allies who know they will ultimately be rivals. Mugabe had had little faith in Nkomo ever since he'd flirted with the internal settlement of Smith and Muzorewa back in the autumn of 1977. Furthermore, Mugabe privately accused Nkomo of not taking a fair share of the war. Mugabe's losses had been much greater in the past few years, and it was no secret that even now Nkomo was keeping back well-trained units in Zambia. Indeed, it was to be one of the most alarming discoveries for the Commonwealth monitoring force that when they arrived in Rhodesia they were to find units of the two men's armies had been fighting for control in certain areas in the weeks leading up to peace – mainly in the south-west near Beitbridge and around the Midlands town of Gwelo.

In the conference to date, the two leaders kept up a show of unity but it was clearly little more than that. For the television cameras they would appear together, Mugabe always uncomfortable, uncharacteristically quiet and subdued in the presence of Nkomo, who seemed to enjoy dominating the interview. On one occasion Mugabe, entering a studio in the basement of Lancaster House and seeing Nkomo waiting for him to join him, backed off saying that he was sure both of them would prefer to be interviewed separately. Realising how embarrassing refusal might be, he did the interview with Nkomo – and then promptly told his publicity man never to allow it to happen again.

The British were all too aware of the tension between the two and there was no doubt that, if Carrington had settled for the second-class solution, he would have tried to get Nkomo in on it. There was a feeling in the Foreign Office that Nkomo was at heart a friend of the British, and that being more 'malleable' than Mugabe, he might bend to the right package. It had always been a major premise in the Carrington strategy that to get Mugabe, Nkomo and Muzorewa in one settlement all three men had to leave Lancaster House believing they would win the election. For no one was that more applicable, the Foreign Office believed, than Joshua Nkomo.

Carrington met Dr Kaunda at Heathrow, concerned about what his message would be, but pleased to see him. The conference needed a catalyst, perhaps 'KK' was the man. The Zambian president said simply that he was worried, profoundly, at the lack of progress at Lancaster House, and then took himself off to the Londonderry Hotel in Park Lane to await the steady stream of callers. Even the leader of Britain's opposition Labour Party, James Callaghan, turned up to say that he felt just like Kaunda. The Government must do the 'honourable thing' and include the Patriotic Front at all costs in any settlement, he said.

At 2.30 that afternoon Mugabe left his apartment, Nkomo his hotel. At three o'clock they were due to give Carrington an answer on the British proposals for the transition, at Lancaster House. But neither had any intention of doing that, or even showing up at the conference at all. They were off to see President Kaunda instead. It was to be one of the comic moments of the conference. Mugabe went to Nkomo's hotel, Nkomo drove to Mugabe's flat, and they missed each other in the wail of police sirens and outriders escorting them. When they finally found each other, in heavy traffic on the Bayswater Road opposite Hyde Park, one of Mugabe's aides told the press: 'Carrington can cool his heels for a while.' The Foreign Secretary was not amused. He was furious, his anger barely veiled in the statement given by his spokesman, Nicholas Fenn, at four o'clock. 'The Chairman,' said Mr Fenn, 'regrets their discourtesy.'

On the seventh floor of the Londonderry hotel, Kaunda heard Mugabe and Nkomo list a series of bitter complaints against the British proposals.

Mugabe said he couldn't accept Salisbury's civil service and police force run the country till elections. 'They are both under the control of men who have been loyal to Smith since the beginning of UDI,' he said. 'Their loyalties, their prejudices will not change and their influence at every level, especially the grass roots, could ruin our chances in an election.'

In reply, Kaunda offered no easy solutions but a simple warning. There was no stomach in Zambia, in Mozambique, in Tanzania for the war any more. That didn't mean peace at any price, but it did mean a lot more give and take by both sides than there had been so far. The conference had come further down the road to a settlement than anything before, he said. Surely there was a way out of the deadlock? Nkomo had expected this counsel of conciliation, Mugabe had not. Perhaps for the first time he realised that he could be going back to war alone. And that was a prospect to sober the most militant on his Central Committee.

That night President Kaunda saw Mrs Thatcher at Downing Street. To her, he also urged compromise. It was no sudden afterthought that he stressed the importance of re-starting maize supplies up through Rhodesia from South Africa to the starving of Zambia. Kenneth Kaunda, said a senior member of the Foreign Office, knew peace could mean his political salvation.

135

The president left three days later, quietly optimistic that Mugabe and Nkomo would agree to peace eventually. He was giving little away on what the compromises were, but it was a clear quid pro quo. Mugabe and Nkomo would have to accept that the civil service in Salisbury provided the only machinery of government for the transition, there was no time to build another. In return, their armies would be given exactly the same status as the forces of Salisbury. Peter Walls would have to keep the peace just like Nkomo and Mugabe.

Ian Smith didn't know the outcome of Kaunda's mediation but his instinct told him what to expect. Flying home to Salisbury on the final day of Kaunda's stay, he gave one of those extraordinary bland and bluff interviews that had become his trademark over the 14 years of UDI. 'I have no doubt that the Patriotic Front will join the settlement,' he said. 'And I must accept that. There's no point in Smithy staying out in the cold. The referee has blown the whistle, the game's over.'

Not quite. It was only four days later that Mugabe, together with Nkomo in a private meeting with Carrington at Lancaster House, relented. It was couched in the dry language of negotiation that Mugabe's precision mind insisted upon. 'In the light of the discussions we have had,' he told the Foreign Secretary, 'if you are prepared to include our forces in Paragraph 13 of the British paper, we are able to agree to the interim proposals.'

Without a trace of the emotion he was feeling, Carrington replied that a sentence would be added to the paragraph in question. It read: 'The Patriotic Front forces will be required to comply with the directions of the governor.'

In that one sentence Mugabe had obtained the legal recognition for his army and, in his own mind at least, for his war, which he had always craved. His men were no longer 'terrorists' or 'guerrillas', they were on an equal footing with the armies of Salisbury. To him, that principle was crucial. One observer was to remark how Mugabe's determination over recognition and status reminded him of the Palestinians, even the Red Brigade in Italy. 'He's almost like the hijacker in the cockpit demanding, first of all, recognition for his cause. Without that, he won't start negotiating. He must have his justification for his war recognised.' Kaunda had also thoughtfully suggested that the guerrillas 'be properly housed and fed'. That also, was to be written into the plans.

'Our forces are now lawful forces,' he said with unmistakable jubilation that night. To which Zvobgo added: 'What more do we want?'

'A lot more,' said Mugabe.

The British were delighted. 'To those of us who have been working at Rhodesia for 14 years, it seems like a miracle,' said one of Carrington's top advisers. General Walls was less enthusiastic. 'It's nonsense to suggest they have equal status with us,' he told journalists. 'If anybody shoots at us, we will stop them from shooting any more.'

The fact was that Carrington was two-thirds of the way home. And the Patriotic Front was still intact

The momentum was now everything, as Nicholas Fenn would tell the Press formally and informally every night. Just as Zvobgo had been beating the drum for Zanu, so did the Foreign Office. Most days Mr Fenn would 'brief' correspondents to the conference. Private sessions in tiny, crowded rooms where they would be given the background information to enable them to broaden their reports beyond the straight verbiage of the conference. Fenn's sharp, agile mind was as much a weapon for Carrington as anything said in conference. Every night now Fenn would assiduously foster the Foreign Office line, realising that come morning Mugabe and Nkomo would be reading the message. The message was 'full speed ahead'. The government would lift sanctions, send the governor, even guillotine the conference, whatever the reaction of Mugabe and Nkomo to the final stage of the conference – the ceasefire arrangements. The tactic of 'take it or leave it' had worked so far for Carrington. The briefings were to add an extra degree of pressure on Mugabe and Nkomo. Every story the press carried saying 'Peace in sight' made it more difficult for them to back out. And Carrington, by this stage, sensed that he had them locked in. His one doubt? Mugabe, always Mugabe. In Carrington's view he would have to be pushed, maybe dragged to peace.

Carrington gave Mugabe and Nkomo six days to mull over his proposals for the ceasefire – then came the ultimatum. Or rather ultimata because there were two of them. On 22 November he said he wanted undertakings within 24 hours from both sides that they would stop cross-border raids from Zambia and Mozambique into Rhodesia, and from Rhodesia into those two countries. By the following Monday, three days away, he wanted a 'yes' or 'no' to the proposals themselves.

Mugabe didn't try to conceal his anger. He stormed out of the conference and told Zvobgo he would handle the media that night. By the time he got to the press room, he was still furious. 'Lord Carrington can go to hell,' he shouted. 'The good Lord is trying to be too clever by half.'

Carrington had known this would be the most difficult stage of the conference. He feared the hostility between the likes of Walls and Tongogara would break out on the conference floor, quickly wrecking all the achievements of the negotiations so far. He'd carefully moved the conference to bilateral talks with the two sides. He would see Salisbury in the morning, the Patriotic Front in the afternoon. It suited Walls, who believed he could forge a deal favourable to his army and government. To an extent it also suited Carrington. Once Salisbury had agreed, he could once again go back to Mugabe and

Nkomo with the second-class solution already assured. It didn't suit Mugabe.

'It is necessary to have direct involvement,' he told the press, calming down now in front of the cameras. 'The two belligerents must talk directly to each other with Britain in the chair. That has not happened.'

Once again came the veiled warning of war if the conference failed. 'Considering the advances we have made in the war, we cannot see them reversed in London at the stroke of a pen, our victory transposed into defeat, General Walls gaining at Lancaster House what he failed to achieve on the battlefield.'

Mugabe refused to even acknowledge the Carrington ultimatum. The only way out of the deadlock was full discussion of the Patriotic Front's own proposals for the ceasefire – for a two-month truce before the election campaign started and a commonwealth peace-keeping force of several thousand men. Mugabe knew that Carrington could not concede either of those cardinal demands. But just as the Foreign Secretary felt he had Mugabe locked in, so Mugabe knew that Carrington could not now countenance the diplomatic failure of not having him in on the settlement. Carrington had also come too far, Mugabe reasoned. It was Mugabe's only card, and he was determined to eke every possible advantage out of it. He turned to the Front Line States once more. The day after Carrington issued his deadlines, Mugabe and Nkomo flew to Dar-es-Salaam for a meeting arranged with the haste that reflected the seriousness of the crisis. As they were en route to Tanzania, the British replied through Mrs Thatcher. 'Nothing,' she said, 'nothing must happen to damage the talks. Success is in sight.'

Mugabe's reaction, on board his Ethiopian airlines flight, was contemptuous dismissal. 'Who is Mrs Thatcher to tell us what to do?' he asked. 'What power does she have in Zimbabwe?' Mugabe was not considering a walk-out, but he did want a show of strength and unity from the Front Line nations to bolster his hand at Lancaster House. He was to get it, but once again with enough reservations to make him realise that a settlement was not just desirable, but imperative.

President Machel arrived before Mugabe and Nkomo, the seriousness of it all emphasised even by his dress – the full military uniform, even cuban heels, he wears only on the most important occasions. He and Nyerere embraced on the tarmac, somehow symbolic of not just the father-son relationship between the two of them, but also the stand they were to take together against the British and the Patriotic Front.

Before the others arrived, Machel and Nyerere had a long session at State House. Mugabe and Nkomo had their support for opposing the British proposals as they stood – but they must accept; if certain concessions were made by the British, particularly if Carrington could strengthen the Commonwealth monitoring force to give it a size equal to the task.

At five o'clock on a sweltering Saturday afternoon the two presidents were joined by Mugabe, Nkomo and envoys from Angola, Botswana and Zambia. Kenneth Kaunda stayed away. He'd put his country on a war footing following Rhodesian raids into Zambia and only that morning had denounced Britain for dealing with Salisbury like 'a spineless hyena'.

In a splendid oak-panelled room overlooking the Indian Ocean, Mugabe put his case. Everything suggested a conspiracy between the Foreign Office and Salisbury, he said. By talking first to Salisbury and then to them, Carrington was showing bias and tended to accept everything Muzorewa and Walls put forward. Yes, they had been given equal status with Salisbury on the armies but they were only words. How could it be equality, he argued, when the Rhodesians would stay where they were and his men would be moved into assembly camps known

140

to the Rhodesians. 'I am not going to stand for my forces being herded like cattle into these detention centres at the mercy of the Rhodesian army and air force. My army could be destroyed within days,' Mugabe said.

Nyerere and Machel, like Kaunda before them, urged conciliation, if not instant concessions from the Front. Machel is reliably reported to have told Mugabe: 'We hear what you are saying, but we know you will hear us when we say the war must end.' At the end of a long meeting, Mugabe remarked only: 'We will be going back to London to negotiate.'

As he and Nkomo flew back to the London winter, Nyerere called British television and radio correspondents, including David Smith, to his home on the beach. Publicly, in the interview he gave Smith, he accused Carrington of 'playing tricks' to secure power for Muzorewa, and warned of the disaster that would follow if the Foreign Secretary failed to pursue an all-party agreement. Privately, he felt that Carrington simply couldn't allow the conference to collapse with the hopes of the international community so high. He was undeniably optimistic, believing both sides would budge enough in the end. 'They both have too much to lose for the conference to fail.'

The next few days saw the conference swing back and forth between disaster and success. On behalf of Lord Carrington, Mr Fenn pursued a confident line couched with a warning. 'The room for manouevre is very small,' he said, 'and there is very little time left. The British delegation remains hopeful of a successful conclusion to this conference.'

Unwittingly perhaps, although Mugabe believed otherwise, Joshua Nkomo fuelled the Foreign Office momentum towards peace. On 30 November, after yet another crisis session with Carrington, he and Mugabe emerged from a side door of the Foreign Office to be greeted by a crowd of pressmen and television cameras. A few

141

cunning questions elicited the quote the media had been led to expect by Mr Fenn's undaunted optimism.

'Agreement is imminent,' said Nkomo.

Mugabe stepped in immediately. 'We can't even pretend we're close to agreement,' he said. But the media, fearing that they had missed the breakthrough, chose largely to ignore Mugabe's remarks. The following day was D-day, for the papers. It was 'yes or no', now or never. Carrington was in Dublin that day with Mrs Thatcher, arguing with the EEC about Britain's contribution to the Common Market. He didn't have much joy there and when he returned to the Foreign Office at six o'clock, ahead of schedule especially for a meeting with the Patriotic Front, there was more bad news from Mugabe.

Instead of an answer, Mugabe had new proposals. He wanted the forces of Peter Walls back in their bases well before his units came in from the bush. Furthermore, he wanted the strongest possible guarantees that the South Africans would withdraw the forces they now admitted having in Rhodesia. At that lunch with Lord Walston in early November, Mugabe had spoken at length about foreign involvement. He said that, from the Patriotic Front's side, there was no threat from Russia or Cuba or China. Only if South Africa entered the conflict might the situation change. In the last week of November the South African prime minister, Pieter Botha, disclosed that he had up to two battalions protecting trade routes in Rhodesia, flying helicopters for the Rhodesian Air Force and providing heavy artillery and logistical support. Without these guarantees, there could be no deal.

Carrington was genuinely shocked. He had expected agreement, instead he was left tantalisingly short of it, so near yet so far. Not for the first time did he acknowledge that in Mugabe he faced not only a fine intellect but a formidable opponent capable of playing him at his own game.

142

The Foreign Office was in deep dismay, partly out of exhaustion, partly because they were victims of their own rhetoric in the previous few days. Suddenly Carrington realised that he might have to go for the second-class solution. And now he was worried about how and if he could mend fences with Mugabe. Mugabe had grown increasingly resentful at what he saw as the Foreign Secretary's high-handed tactics: now, more than ever, he was determined not to be hustled. Carrington sensed that the personal antipathy between them was as responsible as anything for the deadlock. Carrington knew that Mugabe saw him as the aristocrat politician who, by definition, could neither understand nor sympathise with the perceptions and goals of the so-called terrorists. Both men were to recognise that weekend that the conflict of personalities and styles could yet wreck the conference.

Mediation was on its way, though. Not from Lusaka or Dar-es-Salaam, but from Marlborough House, just round the corner from Lancaster House. The secretary-general of the Commonwealth, Shridath 'Sonny' Ramphal, started work that Friday night arguing that the Commonwealth had started the peace process, now it would clinch it. Ramphal had the ear of Nkomo and Mugabe – he'd intervened back in October to remind all that anything but an all-party settlement would be a disaster. A fine lawyer – he drafted the independence constitution for his native Guyana back in 1966 – Ramphal was now to be the devil's advocate to both the Foreign Office and the Patriotic Front. He told Mugabe that his worries about the disposition of the enemy armies in the ceasefire was a matter for the final stage of the conference – there was no point in holding it up if Carrington gave the right assurance about fair play. Mugabe agreed, albeit reluctantly.

But what about the South Africans? Mugabe had by now become almost obsessed by the fear that they would bomb his army once they had arrived in the assembly camps. Ramphal drafted the declaration that was to break the deadlock. 'There will be no external involvement in Rhodesia under the British governor. The position has been made clear to all the Governments concerned.'

'Including South Africa,' Mugabe interjected. 'That must go in.' Nkomo wasn't concerned, he was happy with the insertion as it stood. Ramphal pointed out that Carrington would accept it apart from the specific mention of South Africa. He was right. Carrington was happy enough – he wasn't, after all, being asked for that much. The Rhodesian forces, both on the ground and in the air, would be subject to exactly the same scrutiny and rules as the armies of the Patriotic Front. The monitoring force, from Britain and a handful of Commonwealth countries, would be expanded from the original concept of about 600 to 1200 men to make sure it was big enough for the task. And yes, the Foreign Secretary accepted the importance of precluding any foreign involvement under a British governor. But he baulked at mentioning South Africa, knowing full well that it would anger and embarrass Walls. Walls had gone home agreeing to the ceasefire proposals only on the condition that they weren't changed.

So on three words, 'including South Africa', the conference hung for three days. Mugabe felt he had conceded enough, he wasn't going to budge any more. Carrington believed he could not do it. It was a battle of willpower that threatened everything. The Foreign Office's official line that weekend was that there was no contact with the Patriotic Front. On Monday, Carrington called a full session of the conference. He had to brief the cabinet that night and he wanted an answer from Mugabe and Nkomo.

Mugabe said he had no answer to give. Carrington cancelled the meeting at the shortest notice. He simply

144

let it be known that, if necessary, Britain would go ahead without the Patriotic Front.

By any standards, it was a dangerous gamble. Mugabe called it reckless. In the days to come Carrington was to receive many plaudits for his brinkmanship. But, in the eyes of Mugabe he deliberately induced a serious crisis that Monday. In the words of Ramphal, Mugabe 'dug his heels in for the last fight.' Would the bluff work? Carrington's argument was that it had to work, Mugabe had to be hustled however much he disliked it. There was no other way of getting a settlement. Any further delay could only mean Muzorewa, or more probably Walls, going back on their commitments to the package so far. As Mr Fenn put it, 'the whole thing will begin to unravel like a ball of wool.' That would leave the Foreign Secretary with nothing, not even the second-class solution.

Ramphal appealed to the Foreign Secretary once more, this time stressing that Mugabe would not give in. Wasn't the clause on South Africa a small price to pay for the triumph of a ceasefire? The Foreign Office spoke to Walls and the South Africans. The general was angry, but he knew the tide was running against him. He didn't so much agree with it. He said he'd live with it. Just as on the issue of equal status, Mugabe had won his point of principle. But the concession on the South Africans was his only real gain. The British proposals, apart from a few cosmetics, remained largely unchanged. 'Mugabe won that argument, but he lost the war,' remarked one African diplomat-observer to the conference.

At the session which sealed the ceasefire, Carrington went out of his way to assuage Mugabe. He expressed pleasure with the Front's agreement to the ceasefire, thanked Mugabe personally and praised the 'positive and responsible' way all sides had negotiated. Muzorewa had already gone home. His deputy, Silas Mundawarana, went as far as to call Mugabe and Nkomo 'our brothers in peace'.

Minutes later, Carrington was down in the basement of Lancaster House for the first of the dozen interviews he had scheduled for this, the big day. By the time he reached the television studio – his first call – he was breathless, genuinely excited, admitting that he had still to take it all in. Carrington has often doubted himself in front of the cameras – he worries about projecting himself and his message this way – but tonight he was himself, the adrenalin flowing to produce the occasional chuckle to himself.

'This is a great breakthrough,' he began. 'We have a constitution, we have a transition, and now, we have a ceasefire. That's not bad, is it?'

Could any party turn on it?

'I jolly well hope not. I should hardly think so.'

Did he ever think it was going to fail?

'Two days ago I thought it would fail, I felt there was a great danger of the whole thing collapsing. And I kept thinking what a tragedy it would be if it did collapse because we really had come such a long way.'

Mugabe arrived just as Carrington was finishing. Would he like to sit down for a joint interview with the Foreign Secretary?

'No, I don't think my good Lord Carrington would like that,' he replied.

Mugabe, dapper as always in the dark blue suit he liked for television appearances, had over the weeks become something of a master of the media. He was all too aware of the labels they had pinned on him – 'arch-terrorist', 'hard-line Marxist' – and he tried very consciously to dispel the myth on the screen. He was invariably more relaxed than his interviewers, speaking so softly that he had to be reminded to keep his voice up. He wanted to be heard, listened to, he wasn't going

146

to indulge in shouting matches that would only make him fit the labels.

Tonight he was in good form, clasping the hand of his interviewer and winking as if to say 'what's all the fuss been about?' He even managed to tell the technicians that he hoped Zimbabwe television would have all this 'modern equipment' when he came to power.

He looked a satisfied man. Was he?

'I don't know if I'm satisfied. If I look it its because I'm glad we've got this far, and we're going further to the peace we all want.'

Was he looking forward to elections, did he believe he would win?

'Ah, sure, sure,' he replied with a broad grin. 'Who can win if not our movement? I believe we have done the most mobilisation of the masses during the years of our struggle. Our object in the war was always to create the base for power. We will not be wanting. We have taken care of ourselves in advance.'

Would it be true democracy if he won?

'Yes, sure,' was his answer, followed by a huge sigh as if to ask why do I have to prove I'm a democrat.

'It will be true democracy. This is what we have been fighting for. Power must rest with the people for the people. They must now choose their government, and they will.'

Carrington had refused that night to name his governor but it was little more than an open secret. Christopher Soames, like Carrington a protégé of Macmillan; former war minister, former secretary of agriculture, ex-ambassador to France, and a son-in-law of the late Sir Winston Churchill. He'd been chosen weeks before. As Lord President of the Council, he was announcing cuts in Britain's civil service when he was told that he would be going to Salisbury within four days. Mugabe's response sounded surprisingly hostile, in fact he didn't really believe that the choice of governor would make much difference.

'Lord Soames, Julian Amery, what's the difference?' he asked when told the news.

It was an inauspicious start to a relationship that was to have a decisive influence on the success of putting the Lancaster House agreement into effect.

Soames had never worked in Africa before, his health had been none too strong after a serious heart operation some years before, and some doubted his commitment to whatever job he held. But he was to prove an outstanding choice, his ability to handle a crisis with good humour, patience and principle proving crucial in the months to come. 'I suppose we will simply have to live from hour to hour,' he said on the day his appointment was announced. 'Its not the kind of job to be going into with any preconceived notions, we'll all have to be flexible.'

Nevertheless, Soames had already made his mind up on one or two matters. One was that handling Mugabe was going to be his toughest problem. Two, that Mugabe was the most likely winner.

With Soames, Carrington was to take yet another gamble. The conference was now bogged down over precisely how, where and when the war would end and the ceasefire begin, but Carrington dispatched Soames and his wife Mary to Salisbury. Briefing British journalists himself the same night, he justified the move on the grounds that he still believed Mugabe would have to be pushed over the last hurdle.

The governor, he reasoned, would do three things.

● Keep the momentum going and the pressure on the Patriotic Front.

● Win the new Rhodesia friends in Africa. Those maize supplies so important to President Kaunda could be restarted.

● Stop all Rhodesian raids into Mozambique and

Zambia, so enlisting the good favours of both Machel and Kaunda.

Whatever the logic, it was an audacious step.

Zvobgo, ever the apologist for the cause, was to outline the implications at a press conference just an hour after Soames had left Heathrow airport. 'Make no mistake,' he said (and by now every correspondent recognised those words as the signal to get pen and paper and cameras rolling), 'with the British governor in Salisbury it means a British war against the Patriotic Front.'

To add to the Front's exacerbation, Carrington chose the day of the governor's departure as the moment to present his final plans for the ceasefire, maps and all. The Rhodesians were to have 47 operational bases for their men, the Front 14. You didn't have to be a sooth-sayer to hear Mugabe's cry of 'Foul'. As far as he was concerned, it was merely adding insult to injury that neither he nor Nkomo had been given one camp in the economic heart of the country – the white farmlands in the midlands, ringed by Salisbury in the north-east and Bulawayo in the south-west.

This was the most strategic area in the country, the prime region for white settlements and white farms, for main transport routes, for industry, for towns of any size. Mugabe insisted that his exclusion from the midlands would have a crucial political and psychological impact on his supporters. Guerrillas moving out of the area to camps elsewhere would be seen as signalling ZANLA's defeat. Just as important was the fact that Mugabe and Tongogara did not believe that they would be able to persuade some units to pull out of an area they'd held for so long.

'Do you know who drew these maps,' he remarked that night.

'I'll tell you. Peter Walls.'

Carrington was not to be deterred. He set his final deadline. 11 a.m. on Saturday, 15 December. Then the conference would end, come what may, with or without Mugabe and Nkomo.

Mugabe was not ready for that but he was prepared to call Carrington's bluff one last time. Zvobgo went into what can only be described as battle. Just a few hours from the deadline, on the Friday night, he called every correspondent he could find at Lancaster House. They gathered in the bar, too tired and totally unprepared for the story Zvobgo was to give them.

'Carrington can go to hell,' he shouted. 'Thatcher can jump in the Thames.'

Furthermore: 'Thatcher is in concubinage with Satan Botha.' And, finally, brandishing the British maps and giving a shake of his head directly into camera for each of the television networks there: 'The answer, Lord Carrington, is NO ... NO ... NO.'

Come the deadline, Mugabe began by apologising to Carrington for Zvobgo's immoderate language. That was the only thing he was giving away, because his answer was still NO.

The following morning, Carrington left for Washington with Mrs Thatcher for an official visit. He was quietly hopeful, he said. He was more than that, he firmly expected to come home to hear Mugabe say YES.

Because Lord Carrington already knew that he'd had the final lucky break. And this was a request Mugabe could not refuse.

Fernando Honwana could seem too young for the job he holds. He's 28, and looks no older than that. He was finishing his degree course at York University in England when President Machel came to power in Mozambique in 1975. He flew home, had a short spell of military training in a Frelimo camp, and was immediately put into the president's office as a specialist on Southern Africa affairs. Within a matter of months, he became one of Machel's closest advisers, valued because he'd been educated in the West and understood the West. In the past year, as Machel began to look outside the Soviet bloc for support and economic aid, Honwana's stature had grown immeasurably. He was sent to London to keep the president informed on the conference, and to build bridges with the West.

On the Friday before the deadline Honwana flew into London from Iraq – where Machel was on a State visit. He had an urgent message from his president to Mugabe. It was a letter to a friend, a comrade. But it told Mugabe all too clearly that the war was over. He must accept the peace of Lancaster House, however much it hurt.

Machel had known for some time that his own future was threatened by Mugabe's war. Indeed, he had told Mugabe so in the months before Lancaster House, most clearly at the summit of non-aligned nations in Havana a few weeks before Mugabe came to London.

It wasn't just the burden of tens of thousands of refugees dotted in camps throughout Northern Mozambique, or the flight from the country to the towns sparked off by the Rhodesian raids. For months now, Machel had known that Walls had contingency plans to invade Northern Mozambique and put an end to Mugabe once and for all – if the conference failed. Already there was a so-called Resistance Movement in the North, supported apparently by the Rhodesians and the South Africans. It was no more than an irritant at this stage, but it was a clear indicator of the tactics Salisbury would use if Lancaster House failed.

There had been pressure from the Foreign Office for Machel's intervention. Furthermore, Machel had the example of Kaunda in Zambia. 'The strategy of Smith, the South Africans and the British has been to break Zambia's backbone,' he wrote to Mugabe. If the war resumed Walls would concentrate his attacks on Mozambique, he said. 'We will not be in any position to resist,' Machel wrote. He even mentioned the most likely date for his own fall: July 1980.

His final message was blunt: Mugabe must accept the risk of Lancaster House and fight the elections. He didn't say it but the warning was implicit. Mugabe would have asylum in Mozambique if he refused, but no longer the bases for the war. Mugabe shouldn't have been surprised, but he was ... stunned by the finality of it all.

On Sunday lunchtime he called a meeting of his Central Committee. Mugabe told them they had no option but to accept the Carrington package. The fact that at the same time the Foreign Office was offering a concession – one assembly camp in that economic heartland of the country – was almost academic.

The Mugabes went back to their flat, Sally cooked dinner for him and the Walstons. According to Lord Walston, Mugabe was close to tears throughout the meal.

For a man whose head had ruled his heart for so long, Mugabe had in the end been swayed by the emotional ties of friendship. Coming from anyone else, he would not have believed it. But he knew that Machel did honestly believe that his own revolution would collapse if Lancaster House failed. And that was enough. It was to bring him to peace, but on that Sunday Mugabe did not believe it was to take him to victory.

Chapter 6 — Waiting

It may have been Christmas morning but Mugabe, ever the teetotaller, watched with fatherly disapproval as his aides turned the flight home to Mozambique into a party. They opened up the duty-free whisky they'd bought at London airport, they shouted Zanu slogans, they even broke into a serenade of revolutionary party songs that drowned out the engines on board Air Tanzania flight 511 from Dar-es-Salaam to Maputo.

Eddison Zvobgo asked Mugabe for permission for the 'choir' to go into the cockpit.

'It's all right with me if it's all right with him,' Mugabe said.

Zvobgo and some slightly inebriated colleagues tottered off to the fron of the plane, singing all the way. A few minutes later, Mugabe got up and strolled down the aisle, shaking the hands of every passenger and holding up their babies to kiss. Yes, the election campaign had begun and Mugabe was looking every inch the candidate.

At Maputo airport there was a pleasant surprise for them all. Waiting there, in a long receiving line, was President Machel and most of his Cabinet. From now on Mugabe would be treated here as though he had already won the elections, as though he were a visiting Head of State. It took him about half an hour to embrace not only the Mozambican dignitaries but also every one of the hundreds of Zanu workers who had turned up carrying banners saying 'the struggle continues'.

Mugabe was back in his adopted home. He planned to be here for a matter of days before returning to Salisbury to open his campaign. Instead, he was to be here for five long weeks.

In the final days in London Mugabe would talk about anything – the past, the future, the elections, independence – but he refused point-blank to discuss the Lancaster House agreement. It was not just his deep disappointment with the way he had been forced into it by the Front Line States: rather his belief that he might be destroyed by this peace.

In the last year, his army had embarked on the final stage of the conflict, the 'People's War', as much concerned with organising and educating the people as winning control of towns and villages. With his men now to be in camps, Mugabe felt they would be cut off from the vital task of spreading the word and 'mobilising the masses' during the campaign. They had, Mugabe felt, been deprived of a role in their victory.

But that was not as worrying as Mugabe's real fear that the peace simply would not work. In his own final analysis, he did not believe that Peter Walls and Salisbury would adhere to the ceasefire. The small number of assembly camps and their rural, isolated locations made his men extremely vulnerable to attack. Mugabe believed they would be attacked. More than that, he had a vision of them being bombed by the Rhodesian Air Force. If he had nightmares about it all, he kept them very much to himself. He had had a hard enough time of it convincing the hardliners on his Central Committee, notably Edgar Tekere, to accept the agreement as it was.

When peace was signed in the great hall of Lancaster House on 21 December, his misgivings were all too apparent. Nkomo enjoyed the ceremony hugely, shaking hands enthusiastically with everyone in the room, with General Walls twice.

'You are now our commander,' Nkomo told Walls.

Mugabe studiously avoided Walls and posed reluctantly for the cameras along with Muzorewa, Carrington and Nkomo. Muzorewa seized the opportunity to make the first speech in the election campaign.

If, by 'some terrible miracle,' his party lost, he said, Zimbabwe 'would be finished as far as freedom and democracy and economic development are concerned.'

Mugabe refused to be drawn. He had, he said, only contempt for such 'slander'.

Before going back to Mozambique – and from there on to Rhodesia – there was some important unfinished business. Whether or not Mugabe and Nkomo would fight the election together, or separately. As the Patriotic Front, or Zapu (Nkomo) and Zanu (Mugabe). In the final few days in London, the two men had been unable to resolve that question. Now Mugabe and his Central Committee were to decide for both of them by electing to go it alone.

On the face of it, it was a dangerous gamble. Together they did look invincible. Nkomo, the father of Rhodesian nationalism as his campaign was to proclaim; Mugabe, the guerrilla leader whose army had born the brunt of the fighting that had forced Smith to settle. For Mugabe, there were advantages. Nkomo was much better known inside the country than him and, despite the furore over the attacks on the Viscounts by Nkomo's men, was generally thought to be much more of a moderate. Furthermore, they could potentially divide the country electorally between them. Nkomo would surely take all in his native Matabeleland, while Mugabe could expect to match, if not outpoll, Muzorewa among the Shona tribe around Salisbury and all along the eastern border with Mozambique.

Nkomo had never made any secret of his belief they should fight the election together – 'united we stand, divided we might fall,' he sometimes admitted. But he did have a price for it.

As the veteran of the independence struggle, he argued, he must surely become prime minister in the wake of victory. Mugabe and key members of his Central Committee found that hard to stomach. All of them, in fact, except Josiah Tongogara.

Tongogara, in the final week in London, had argued time and again for a joint campaign with Nkomo. There was more to it than just the expediency of going to the polls with the best possible chance. At Lancaster House, Tongogara had come to respect, indeed admire, Nkomo's political know-how and cunning.

They met several times alone during the conference, with Nkomo making strong overtures about the necessity for the Patriotic Front to stay intact for the election, even hinting at the kind of seniority in government Tongogara would enjoy under him. Tongogara was not swayed by the suggestion of a top post. He had never seen himself as a politician, rather the kingmaker of them. He preferred to keep the talks focused on the campaign and plans for his army to join forces, integrate with Nkomo's once the ceasefire was in force.

They got on well, both men realising that they were a lot closer than they had ever imagined. Tongogara was impressed by Nkomo's platform for a joint campaign and he had become increasingly convinced that without it Mugabe and Zanu ran a grave risk of being kept out of power, as Tongogara knew that Nkomo might be tempted into an anti-Mugabe alliance that would include Muzorewa and the whites. Characteristically, Mugabe let the debate run its course inside his own Central Committee. Now more than ever, he opted for committee decision, collegiate style leadership, rather than making his own independent choice and pushing it through. In the past it had often made for indecision, now it was to produce a quick, decisive move. Tongogara was outvoted overwhelmingly. Tekere, Muzenda, Zvobgo, Sally, all decried the idea that Nkomo would be an asset. Many of their supporters, they argued, hated Nkomo because he had entertained the idea of a deal with Smith in the past. A joint 'Nkomo–Mugabe' ticket could pull less votes than Zanu alone, perhaps prompt many to vote for Muzorewa, especially in Mashonaland.

By the time Mugabe and his delegation left London on 22 December the matter seemed to have been settled. One of Mugabe's closest aides, careful to insist that his remarks should not be attributed to him, said: 'People will say why should we vote for Mugabe if it means that we will vote for Nkomo as well. That is why we will campaign as Zanu and not as the Patriotic Front. If we are tied to Nkomo, people will vote for Muzorewa.'

The first stop was Dar-es-Salaam for a meeting with the Front Line States. And there Mugabe ran into opposition immediately for his independent campaign.

Over the years, President Nyerere and his fellow Front Line leaders had painstakingly nurtured and established the Patriotic Front. Often he had heard recriminations from Mugabe and Nkomo about each other. Just as often he had counselled unity and forgiveness. Nyerere was not just unhappy about the split, he was positively frightened of the consequences. Running separate campaigns would divide the nationalist vote and help Muzorewa.

'You could be playing into Muzorewa's hands,' Nyerere told Mugabe.

Mugabe failed to convince Nyerere with his belief (and that of his committee) that Zanu's support might be seriously eroded by a formal alliance with Nkomo. But he promised to have the Central Committee consider it once more when they all got home to Maputo.

That was not the only hitch during the short stop-over in Dar-es-Salaam. Some of Mugabe's most senior men did not try to conceal their anger at the moves made by Nyerere and Machel to persuade them into signing the peace agreement. They had, they said to anyone who would listen, been 'railroaded' into abandoning the war and agreeing to peace. Mugabe was cautious, carefully avoiding any trace of resentment.

'We have been making the best of circumstances not

of our choosing for more than a decade and we'll make the best of present circumstances,' he said as he left Tanzania.

Despite the party on board the plane, the Central Committee got little sleep on return to Mozambique. They were in almost continuous session, more than one meeting lasted through the night. Again Tongogara argued for a coalition with Nkomo, this time he could call on Machel and Nyerere for support. Again the hardliners opposed him, now more determined than ever to defy the presidents who had forced them into agreement back in London.

Over this, the Christmas holiday, Nkomo sent a delegation from Zambia to talk to Zanu. They carried warnings of 'election failure' if the two parties did not stay together. As always Mugabe was careful not to insist, refusing to be rushed and rush his committee. He did make it clear, in one all-night session, that he preferred to campaign alone. It was the crucial factor, and Nkomo's team went home empty-handed.

At that same session, Tongogara made his final plea for dropping the name Zapu and Zanu and running simply as the Patriotic Front. The war, he said, had not been about personalities or parties but the removal of discrimination and oppression.

To a silence that was rare in any of their meetings, Tongogara insisted that it would be ridiculous for Zanu to refuse to consider Nkomo as a leader of the Front after they had sat down and negotiated alongside him for 14 weeks in London.

Tongogara knew then that he'd lost. He was more disappointed than angry and did not resist when he was dispatched – before the meeting which formally took the decision to campaign alone – to guerrilla camps in central and northern Mozambique to explain the Lancaster House agreement and the election strategy to guerrilla commanders. Mugabe saw Tongogara off from his home in Maputo. It was the last time he was to see him alive.

News of Tongogara's death in a road accident reached Maputo with a call from a Mozambican official stationed near the northern port of Beira to Mugabe's deputy, Simon Muzenda. The official spoke no English, Muzenda little Portuguese, and the line was bad.

Nevertheless, Muzenda got the gist of it all.

Tongogara's Mercedes had crashed into the back of a truck while it was trying to overtake a lorry on a notoriously poor, bumpy road near the town of Palmeira about 100 miles north of Maputo. It was pitch dark at the time of the accident and the truck which they hit did not have its lights on.

Tongogara, who was sitting in the front passenger seat, had been decapitated as he was hurled through the windscreen on impact. His driver was seriously injured, the official said. Muzenda tried to call Mugabe. But by then he was on his way to President Machel's home. The president had called him personally and told him to come at once. Machel was close to tears as he gave Mugabe the news. He had always felt a great personal attachment to Mugabe's general, perhaps more than for Mugabe himself.

Mugabe was clearly distressed when he called at the British Embassy a few hours later. He did not suspect foul play, he said.

He had already told the Central Committee that he would personally supervise the funeral arrangements. His attempts to get the body back to Maputo quickly turned into a fiasco that served only to fuel the suspicion and rumours that Tongogara had been murdered.

A Mozambican government plane was sent to pick up the body. But when the pilot landed at a small airstrip in central Mozambique, near the scene of the crash, he found there was no fuel for the return trip. The plane had to stay where it was. His message did not reach

Maputo till the next day, when a land rover was sent. It was more than two days before Tongogara's body reached Maputo and the mortuary.

The suspicions of murder – to which the Rhodesians, the British, and even Nkomo were to admit – were inevitable. They were even aroused among Mugabe's own troops. Most of them, inside Rhodesia, first heard the news on a Rhodesian Broadcasting news bulletin which referred to them as 'terrorists'. It hardly seemed credible that Tongogara, the arch-opponent of splitting the Patriotic Front, the man who had pursued an independent dialogue with Nkomo and the only strong voice of dissent on the Central Committee should die in such circumstances at such a vital stage. Just three days after Christmas, he was due to have been in Salisbury to oversee the assembling of his guerrillas and address them in the camps where they would stay.

Privately, the British were dismayed. Tongogara had surprised them at Lancaster House with his emergence as a leader who looked beyond partisan interests. They feared that his death would jeaopardise not only the immediate ceasefire but the stability of the country in the future.

Those at Government House who believed there had been a plot were later to point to the fact that Rex Nhongo, Tongogara's successor, issued specific orders for hundreds of guerrillas to stay out of the camps during the election campaign. They also painted a grim scenario of the Patriotic Front without Tongogara.

The one man who was capable of bringing Mugabe and Nkomo together, of forming one army from their two, had gone. The likelihood of civil war remained, they argued.

The fact is that Mugabe himself was genuinely shocked and upset. On the night the news reached Maputo, he went to the Tongogara home and spent the whole night with his family. When the body arrived, he took Tongogara's widow to the mortuary and then arranged for a white Rhodesian mortician, a long-time friend of Zanu, to be flown in from Salisbury to embalm the corpse. Mugabe knew the world at large would conclude 'murder'. He called the few foreign correspondents in Maputo to his home. 'There was no split between myself, or any other Zanu leaders, and Tongo,' he said.

'I admit that Tongo was always looking for ways to heal the rift between Zanu and Zapu and was one of the few people who commanded respect of Zanu militants.

'But Tongo, like everyone else on the Central Committee, saw the need for Zanu to go it alone in the elections.'

Statements like that did not dispel the suspicion that Tongogara had been murdered. They did, however, lead some Western diplomats who presumed murder to say that, if there was a plot, Mugabe was probably ignorant of it.

The fact is that all the evidence gathered – and some Western embassies managed to get their own version of what happened – suggests that it was a genuine accident.

For two days Tongogara's body lay in state at the Maputo hospital mortuary. On 2 January, as the first of his men began to arrive in any numbers at assembly camps in eastern Rhodesia, he was buried.

Mugabe led the mourners in filing past the coffin in a tiny room at the mortuary. Behind him came dozens of Zanu guerrillas in army fatigues, behind them followed dozens more in wheelchairs, the wounded from the war. As they passed by the open casket, they sang party songs and raised their fists to chant 'Zanu'. Mugabe was close to tears as he watched the crippled pass, but retained his composure enough to keep the line moving fairly swiftly.

Samora Machel had been expected at the mortuary, instead he sent word that he was going direct to the cemetery. The Zanu militants crowded into the few cars and trucks available to them, Tongogara's coffin in a

Mercedes at the head of the procession. Hundreds of Mozambicans lined the streets, bowing their heads as the entourage passed.

At the cemetery gates Machel and Mugabe embraced, then led the cortège into a small hall where the ceremony was held. There was no service and barely enough room for the Central Committee, the Mozambican Cabinet and the dozens of diplomats who had come to pay their respects. Mugabe and Machel placed their own private wreaths on the coffin, followed by ambassadors from almost every African State.

Mugabe's address was delivered in his usual soft-spoken, low-key way. Tongogara, he said, had been the founding father of the liberation movement, he had created the Zanla army. He would be impossible to replace but, despite the loss, the struggle would continue.

Machel was anything but low-key. 'Farewell, Comrade Tongogara,' he cried at the beginning of his emotional eulogy.

The president spoke in Portuguese and even those, like Mugabe, who didn't speak the language quickly understood the main thrust of his address.

His eulogy was both a pledge to Tongogara, 'a dear friend and comrade,' and a lecture to the Central Committee of Zanu. Tongogara, he said, had spent his whole life seeking unity among the liberation forces.

'I call on all those present,' Machel said, 'to honour the memory of comrade Tongogara by now making unity a reality.'

It was too late for that but it was not too late for Machel to play a vital role in persuading Mugabe that moderation would now be the key to victory.

To those who have met both men, the most striking similarity between Machel and Mugabe lies in the razor-sharp quality of their minds. Interestingly, they were both educated as youngsters by Catholics. Then their two paths split absolutely. Mugabe went into teaching, then prison, developing into an ideologue during the years he spent in detention. Machel's Marxism was nurtured and grew as he led Frelimo's war against the Portuguese, rather than through the literature which had converted Mugabe. 'War is the best university.' Machel likes to say.

The priests who taught Machel as a boy wanted him to go into the priesthood but he refused. Instead he became a nurse. As such he travelled widely in Mozambique and most of what he saw angered and dismayed him. In 1961 he joined Frelimo and went for training in Algeria. When he returned, he was to lead Frelimo both militarily and ideologically. In the late 1960s Frelimo was strongly anti-white. The guerrilla army recruited largely through their pledge to destroy the Portuguese who had exploited and abused the African. Machel, as a nurse, had found discrimination at every level of society – even in his skilled capacity, whites were earning several times more for doing the same job as him.

But Machel was already looking beyond the short-term needs of the armed struggle, to the day when Frelimo would take over, and when the great debate within the movement started over whether Frelimo was engaged in a race or a class war, he was at the forefront of those commanders who argued against racism.

Black nationalism could be just as exploitive as white colonialism, he argued. Frelimo must not be racist, instead it had to crush racism in Mozambique.

Machel won and from then Frelimo was committed to defeating colonialism, rather than the whites. Frelimo, unlike most other African revolutionary parties has attracted a growing number of whites, Asians and coloureds. Whites were brought into the cabinet in 1980.

It was an important distinction, just the same as that made by Tongogara when he talked about Ian Smith and his mother at the beginning of the Lancaster House conference. Both Tongogara and Mugabe had learned it from Machel during the years of exile in Mozambique – and Mugabe was now to pin his bid for power firmly on the same principle.

Machel himself defined their common enemy in 1977, when most of the whites had already fled and the president was left to rue the day they did. 'Colonialism is a permanent crime against humanity – a cancer which corrodes daily, nourished by the blood of the poor and oppressed.

'Racism is a permanent crime against mankind, depriving man of his personality and dignity, humiliating him to the point where he believes he is inferior because of the colour of his skin. It is hard for outsiders to imagine how we suffered – even wishing that we had been born with a different-coloured skin from that of our parents. Why was I born with such an unfortunate colour? Only coloured people can really understand the permanent affront to our human dignity.

'Now here in Mozambique we have established real equality between men. It is from this so many Portuguese are running away. They cannot face up to real racist equality. We are the most obdurate and uncompromising enemies of racism. But we also feel that by putting too much stress on the apartheid issue the danger is that revolutionary forces may be diverted into waging an anti-white campaign.

'That is why we say let us define the enemy.

'It is not the whites, it is not a question of skin pigmentation.

'It is, in our area of the world, colonialist capitalist oppression.'

For Machel and Mozambique, such a candid declaration of the enemy and goals had come too late. The damage had been done in the last few months before independence, when the Portuguese settlers fled in droves in anticipation of Frelimo atrocities. Its never been established whether their flight was simple panic or the result of intimidation or coercion by Frelimo. Certainly there was little visible evidence of harrassment of the whites, few had homes attacked, even less had possessions stolen.

Most likely they were simply scared by the onward march of a revolution that trumpeted its 'Marxismo-Leninismo'. The white specialists – engineers, agronomists, doctors – felt they had been forewarned by the tone and nature of Frelimo to expect that they would be 'nationalised' overnight. The exodus of a quarter of a million Portuguese was underway before Frelimo could do anything to reverse it.

Machel, more than anybody, had come to regret that. At independence he inherited a country bankrupt of educated, skilled labour because the Portuguese had carefully ensured that only the whites were trained to any professional level. The statistics tell the story. On 25 July 1975, independence day in the re-named capital of Maputo, Machel had 2 Mozambican engineers, 3 agronomists, 5 vets and 36 doctors. For a population of 12 million.

As he tried to give his people the basics his revolution had promised them – food, clothing, education, work, medical treatment – Machel recognised time and again the vacuum left by the white exodus.

Furthermore, as the president was fond of saying, it wasn't just their departure that threatened his revolution, it was also the manner of it. One of his close aides put it like this:

'It's not just that the Portuguese went. It's that when they did they destroyed everything they had, they left us nothing. If they wrecked a tractor, they also burned the manual that made sure we couldn't put it back together.'

Five years on, Machel was still suffering the consequences of a war that had been perceived by the white community to have been racist.

Those consequences were all too visible in the Maputo

that Mugabe returned to from London.

It wasn't just the dilapidated state of the city, or the long queues for the few foodstuffs and goods on sale at the few shops open, even the fact that the revolutionary wall murals needed a coat of paint. The country at large was facing deep decay, the revolution was at the crossroads.

Down on the hundreds of collective, state farms, for example. Lacking the equipment and expertise, they were nowhere near production levels of pre-independence days. Mozambique, which should be a major food exporter, had to import huge quantities of basic foods.

As a result, the balance of payments deficit in 1979 had reached 230 million dollars, more than the country's total exports in 1978. It would have been twice that had it not been for a substantial amount of foreign aid, notably from Sweden.

Figures like that – with no likely improvement on the horizon – had made peace imperative for Machel. And with peace, came a respite for his revolution.

The president used it to go on the offensive with his own people back home.

In early December, as Mugabe was inching slowly towards peace in London, Machel made the first of a major series of speeches designed to make Mozambicans recognise their own failings. It was a fundamental change of tactics by the president. He wanted to shock his people out of the bureaucracy, apathy and inefficiency that could wreck both him and the revolution.

Beneath the jargon there was a sharp message for everyone. 'I will not have opportunists and petty bourgeois radicals trying to break down authority with ultra-democracy and leftism,' he said. 'They are creating a false egalitarianism where unskilled men and women have moved into jobs for which they are not fit. They are so debilitating the entire economy.'

Within a few weeks the jargon was translated into action. And dramatic change.

Out, for example, went the national chain of 'people's shops', which had handled food and clothing and had been such a dismal failure. Those who ran them (and were paid more than nurses, Preisdent Machel noted) had done little to find goods to sell, so their shops were often empty. In such circumstances it was 'Leftism' to deny a role to private traders, it had been a mistake to take over small businesses as the government had. Within a few weeks Machel was saying: 'The state will create the conditions to support private traders, farmers and industrialists. Private activity has an important role to play in straightening out our country.'

He followed it up with daily visits to shops, factories, farms, power stations, even Maputo airport, to personally urge workers to get rid of incompetence, corruption and sloth. It meant that by the time Mugabe got back from London Machel was not only advocating the politics of pragmatism, he was practising it. His change in tactics and the advice he was now to give was to have a profound effect on Mugabe as he prepared to go home to Zimbabwe to campaign.

On 9 January Machel took up a long-standing invitation to speak to Mugabe's Central Committee in Maputo. They were busy at work on their manifesto for the elections. Once again Mugabe allowed the fullest possible debate of every issue. And once again the hardliners pushed the militant line: a full-blooded Marxist programme that would have included large-scale nationalisation, the immediate transfer of land from the whites to the Africans, even the breaking of ties with South Africa.

President Machel's intervention, as the voice of moderation and pragmatism, was decisive.

It was no secret that for some time Machel and his senior aides had doubted Zanu's commitment to

Marxism. It wasn't that they queried the ideology, rather that they believed Mugabe and his Central Committee had never had the time and the freedom to create a united party line that a Marxist State required. There had, they said, been too many wrangles, too many purges, too many personal rivalries within Zanu for the party to define its direction. In these circumstances, Machel believed it would be extremely dangerous for Zanu to even talk about Marxism: it was a goal they could never achieve with any disunity at the top and to talk of it would only serve to panic white Rhodesians.

It was the whites who were uppermost in the president's mind when he addressed the Central Committee. There was, he said, a clear distinction between the 'lackadaisical, corrupt and cruel' Portuguese colonials and the whites in Rhodesia. The Rhodesian whites, whatever their failings, had much to offer the new Zimbabwe in building the economy after independence. He offered the Mozambican example. He, more than anyone, knew how catastrophic a white exodus could be. 'Cut out the rhetoric because you will scare the whites away and you need them,' Machel said. 'You will face ruin if you force the whites there into precipitate flight.'

According to Mozambican sources, Machel turned to the ideology of the party as it prepared for the elections. It was a remarkable display of candour and common sense.

'Don't try to imitate us,' he said. 'Don't play make-believe Marxist games when you get home. You have no Marxist party as yet, so you can't create Marxism.

'It's difficult enough in Mozambique and we are a Marxist party.'

The mood inside Mugabe's party leadership changed instantly. The message of moderation in the manifesto produced a few days later was all too evident.

There was not a mention of Marxism, indeed only a passing reference to socialism. From the issue of the

168

whites, through industry, to agriculture, education, even religion, the manifesto reflected a leadership trying to compromise ideology with reality: and assimilate and learn from the problems encountered and the mistakes made by the Mozambicans. It did envisage 'socialist transformation'.

'In working towards the socialist transformation of Zimbabwean society,' the manifesto said, 'a Zanu government will ... recognise historical, social and other existing practical realities of Zimbabwe. One of these existing practical realities is the capitalist system which cannot be transformed overnight. Hence, while a socialist transformation process will be brought underway in many areas of the existing economic sectors, it is recognised that private enterprise will have to continue until circumstances are ripe for socialist change.'

In conclusion, Mugabe and his party put themselves in the front line in the battle against racism, just as Machel had done years earlier. Unlike Machel, Mugabe had the opportunity to persuade the whites to stay and he was determined to seize it.

'Zanu wishes to give the fullest assurance to the white community, the Asian and coloured communities that a Zanu government can never in principle or in social or government practice, discriminate against them. Racism, whether practised by whites or blacks, is anathema to the humanitarian philosophy of Zanu. It is as primitive a dogma as tribalism or regionalism. Zimbabwe cannot just be a country of blacks. It is and should remain our country, all of us together.

'Let us thus work together and build a nation, united and strong.'

The British were fully aware of the advice President Machel was giving Mugabe. But still the barrier of distrust kept Government House in Salisbury and Mugabe apart. They distrusted his commitment, just as he did theirs. This mutual distrust was to keep Mugabe in Mozambique till three weeks after Machel's speech.

The Rhodesian air force had not bombed his men, but now Mugabe feared something wholly more machiavellian: that Britain's real objective was to protect its own economic and political interests by ensuring the emergence of a moderate, pro-Western government, which would have no hesitation in crushing his revolution.

First came word from Lord Soames in Salisbury that since other politicians, among them Bishop Muzorewa and the Reverend Sithole, wanted to hold rallies in the capital on the Sundays Mugabe planned to return, he could not come back on those days. Nkomo had returned on 12 January to a huge crowd. Mugabe did not wish to be seen to attract less than Nkomo or Muzorewa. The only day his supporters could all turn out would be a Sunday. The governor's argument was simple – the police could not guarantee law and order if two rival parties held rallies in the same place on the same day: and his rivals had booked ahead of him. Then followed a demand from the governor that Mugabe have 71 political opponents, 'dissidents', purged from Zanu two years earlier, released from jails in Mozambique. Mugabe, said Lord Soames, could not come home until the likes of Herbert Hamadziripi and Rugare Gumbo had been freed.

This came quickly after news from Salisbury that a handful of guerrillas had been killed by the Rhodesian security forces for failing to report to the assembly camps, and the announcement from Salisbury that Lord Soames had agreed to allow a small number of South African troops to be stationed inside Rhodesia, protecting vital road and rail links like Beitbridge across the Limpopo river.

Mugabe smelt a conspiracy.

When he spoke to David Smith in Maputo on 14 January he gave full voice to his theory of a plot. 'The British are working against us, working against us on two

170

fronts. First the military front, where they are dishonouring the ceasefire. They've never actually ensured that the Rhodesians have disengaged, they have now gone back on their assurances that South African troops would remove themselves from the country. And they are now hounding up our forces, shooting them callously without giving them a chance to move to the assembly camps even though there was not enough time for them to be informed about the ceasefire and to be taken to the camps.

'On the political front, Britain is delaying our departure here under all kinds of false excuses. One excuse given us was that Muzorewa was holding a rally one weekend and we couldn't get our people into Salisbury. Just because Muzorewa was holding his own rally.

'I couldn't believe that Lord Soames could act in a manner which would obviously show that he was pro-Muzorewa and against us.'

Smith: Do you still have faith in the British?

Mugabe: No, no, I ... I ... I just have lost ... I mean I have no faith in them, I have just lost every ounce of faith I had in the British Government. I never knew they were capable of this dishonesty. It's really shocking.

Smith: Do you believe you can still win?

Mugabe: Ah, yes, sure, sure, sure, the evidence is all there. We have full support throughout the country, we believe our calculations will be proved correct.

Smith: You talk of evidence, what evidence?

Mugabe: Evidence? Evidence of support. Talk to the ordinary man in the street and he will tell you he supports us. Talk to the rural people, the peasants, and they will tell you that by and large they support us. We don't need any more. And the reason why the British Government and the Rhodesian forces are hounding up our forces and making it difficult for us generally is that they realise that we are going to win and they want to place every obstacle in our way to prevent that.

171

However strongly Mugabe may have believed there was a conspiracy against him, his belief in himself and his party was stronger. Now that the hurdle of the cease-fire had been crossed – without the Rhodesians destroying his army – he was convinced he would win the election. That's why he gave way when Machel insisted that the detainees be released and that he return immediately on the first Sunday 'free'.

A few days after that interview with Smith, Sally Mugabe wrote to Lady Walston. 'At last it seems we can go back home soon. We planned to leave earlier but the Governor has sent a message saying we can't. Mind you, there will only be one month to elections. All the others have been allowed in and are actively campaigning, some openly supported by this governor...

'We are totally disappointed about his biased stance. Conditions are so hard for us, even now that the country has returned to so-called legality. We shall in spite of all this carry on and with the help and support of broad masses of the people who stand solidly behind us, we shall overcome ... if his lordship governor Soames allows it.'

In the final 10 days of exile, Mugabe had the time for something he had always promised himself: the study, the reading, the policy discussions that he knew he needed if he were to be an effective prime minister. He had been doing it on and off for years but before it had always been a distant prospect.

To the few visitors he received in those last few days in Mozambique, he was a man transformed. He was not concerned, as he had been for years, with the decision of the moment, the politics of today, the latest news from Salisbury: rather the politics of tomorrow, Zimbabwe under his rule, the problems he would face. He read almost everything he could find on Rhodesia. Industry in particular preoccupied him, especially the mines. The mines were almost wholly in the hands of the private sector. He did not want to nationalise them, but he did

172

want more State involvement, he said – not just to reap profits but to improve the lot of the people who worked them.

He reeled off the frightening statistics that accompanied the problems facing a new government in Zimbabwe: a million people uprooted from their homes, it was already too late for them to go home and sow the crops to feed themselves this year; nearly half a million children without schools which had been closed because of the war; just a handful of doctors still working out in the rural areas, serving millions of people.

Mugabe was, in short, reading himself in to be prime minister. It wasn't just the knowledge that the 'People's War' had sewn up the vote in large areas of the country that made him so certain of victory. Nor was he a victim of his own rhetoric. And he certainly wasn't naive enough to believe that because he was the most able, he would win.

Mugabe had unshakeable, almost religious faith in the justness of his cause. Without the war, there would have been no Lancaster House, no compromise from Smith and Walls, no chance in his lifetime for a free and fair Zimbabwe. The people would recognise that, most of them did already. And they would listen to him when he said, 'we fought the war to win the peace.' Of that he was sure.

Chapter 7 — The Election

Mugabe hadn't slept well for years. It was a legacy of the time in prison. This night was no exception. He managed just a couple of hours sleep and by 4.30 in the morning he was up at the house in Maputo for his usual hour of calisthenics, exercises and meditation. He couldn't face any breakfast. It was the day he'd been waiting for all his life but, as he was to admit later, he was too excited to really enjoy it.

By 7.30 a.m. he and Sally were at Maputo's Mavalane airport. A Boeing 727 of Deta, the State carrier, was waiting for them. Only a few months before Mozambique barely had an airline, now a British company (British Midland Airways) had been contracted to provide the planes, the pilots and the technicians. Travelling back as well were 100-odd Zanu workers, many of whom had spent five years in Mozambique like the Mugabes. They had followed him into exile. Now they were following him home to Zimbabwe.

It was 90 minutes to Salisbury, just an hour and a half for him to prepare for the biggest challenge of his career. He spent most of the time running over the statement he was to give the press on touch-down. He knew it would be crucial to his chances, it was vital to create the right impression from the outset. Nkomo, after all, was already two weeks into his campaign, Muzorewa had been campaigning for months. Occasionally he looked out of the window, reflecting in a matter of seconds upon all that had happened in the past. The 11 years in detention, the loss of the children he never knew, the years of war, the bitter peace of Lancaster House. All that, he told himself, had been building towards this – the moment when he would come home to Zimbabwe, 'the bloodthirsty Communist terrorist' to some, the hero to others.

The plane touched down at 9.30 a.m. Salisbury airport was deserted, just a few members of the monitoring force waiting in their tents on the edge of the runway, waiting not for Mugabe but for RAF cargo planes due in later with supplies and equipment.

The governor had banned all demonstrations at the airport for 'homecomings' ever since Rex Nhongo and other Zanla commanders had returned on 26 December. Tens of thousands of Patriotic Front supporters had turned out to lay siege to the airport, the police had moved in with dogs, and there were many arrests. The governor wanted to avoid confrontation like that, hence the ban.

The Mugabes were first down the steps, waving to the small crowd – almost all of them pressmen – up on the balcony of the terminal. Mugabe strode towards the terminal, bounding along as if he couldn't wait to get the formalities over with. There was no VIP treatment, they had to clear customs and immigration like everyone else. Coming through the terminal, a white airport worker swore at them, not to their faces but within earshot, loud enough for them to know what he thought. Three months later, with Mugabe elected, Sally recalled that moment.

'Now when I go to airport, I am escorted in VIP fashion,' she wrote to Elizabeth Walston on 1 May 1980. 'But only three months ago, January 27, when we arrived after five years of exile for Robert and 17 for me, I was rough handled and was told a lot of insulting words by the white airport staff. They are the very ones escorting me now. Was that behaviour necessary at all?'

The press room at the airport was tiny, and dozens of newsmen crowded in to hear Mugabe. Zvobgo, as always, produced a line to fit the occasion.

'Ladies and gentlemen, it's my great pleasure to present – not present, introduce to you again – the next prime minister of the free Zimbabwe, Robert Gabriel Mugabe.'

175

Mugabe knew many of the faces he was addressing – from Dar-es-Salaam, Maputo, Lusaka, Rome, Stockholm, Geneva, Lancaster House, the stopping-points of what had seemed like a lifetime in exile.

'Fancy seeing you *here*,' he remarkedly pointedly to one British correspondent. He had, after all, given very few press conferences in Salisbury.

The statement was a model of precision. Thanks to censorship few Rhodesians, white or black, had ever seen Mugabe before. He knew that for the first time the papers, television and radio would report what he said – and report it as the statement of an election candidate not 'terrorist'.

He weighed every word heavily, frequently looking at his audience to make sure they were listening and to see how they reacted. For many Rhodesians, watching him on television that night, this was a new Mugabe, not the Mugabe they'd been told about. But anyone who had followed him in the previous few months recognised the thoughtful, intelligent, articulate politician who had negotiated so skilfully at Lancaster House. He had an impassioned statement of moderation and peace, trying to allay the fears of all Rhodesians and dispel the thing that could damage him most – the myth built up around his very name. 'The State of Zimbabwe must be truly democratic,' he said. 'In other words, there must be a complete reversal of the situation where you have "equals" and "unequals", superiors and inferiors, whites and blacks.

'We shall reverse that. But we shall not create out of the majority an oppressive race. We shall attain equality through democracy, where there won't be any discrimination on the basis of race and colour.

'We are pledged to that type of democracy. We are pledged to giving everybody, regardless of race and colour, a place in society. There is, therefore, no need for anxiety or fear. We mean what we say.

'We were honest in the struggle, fought gallantly for what we considered were our honest objectives, and we shall be honest in peace to achieve a society where all will have a place.

'This is our goal.'

They started arriving shortly after dawn. A few had come by car, hundreds by bike, thousands by bus. Tens of thousands more had walked. By 11 o'clock that morning Zimbabwe grounds in the township of Highfields was not just packed, it was overflowing. They carried banners saying 'Viva Mugabe' and 'Lotta continua', they wore tee-shirts emblazoned with the cockerel symbol of Zanu (PF), and they held portraits of the man above their heads. Suddenly, Mugabe's comment 10 days earlier about the strength of his support didn't sound like election rhetoric.

They had their marshals, rigorously body-cheling everyone at the gates. They had their own first-aid units, handling the dozens who fainted in the heat. And they had their own choir, keeping up an endless rendition of the Zanu anthem, 'Zimbabwe'.

Mugabe was late, but no one cared. When his white Mercedes pulled into the grounds up behind the rostrum, dozens of supporters threw themselves over the bonnet, climbed on the roof. He didn't so much climb the steps at the back of the stage, he was swept along by the tide, lifted off his feet. By now his eyes were moist with a few private tears. He'd lost Sally, she was back among the throng surrounding the car. When he reached the podium, 200,000 voices were raised as one, screaming, 'Mugabe, Mugabe, Mugabe.' For five minutes they kept it up, this Zimbabwean standing ovation, Mugabe raised both hands above his head like some gladiator, turning in full circle to each section of the crowd and bowing. The public figure beamed a huge smile, the private man cried a little. When it finally died down, his first words were a long litany of the allies who had brought him to this moment of triumph.

'Long Live President Nyerere,' he shouted over the loudspeaker system.

'Long Live President Kaunda.'

'Long Live President Samora Machel, Long Live Mozambique!'

He paused, telling, ordering the crowd to hush as though he'd been practising all his life.

'And never forget the comrades who have fallen. A Lotta Continua!' The crowd was silent for a few seconds, then it erupted into long and loud applause.

Mugabe was home. And he had four weeks to win an election he'd been preparing for for over 20 years.

The evidence had been building up over the weeks. Throughout January. A report from a police station in Gwelo, a phone call from an election commissioner in Umtali, a personal visit to Government House from a party official. All pointed to the same thing – the kind of serious intimidation that could make a farce of the elections.

Sooner or later they would end up on the desk of Sir John Boynton, the election commissioner, or his deputy Malcolm Carruthers. And sooner rather than later they passed them on to the governor.

From the moment he had arrived in mid-December, Lord Soames had realised that intimidation was the one unknown factor that could not only wreck the chances of peace but also create the conditions for civil war – under his authority.

As early as 22 December, Lord Soames had been given a first warning. At 9.45 that morning a blue Peugeot drove past the house of Mugabe's sister in Highfields. At the end of the road it turned round and cruised slowly back past the house. Two Africans in the car opened up with automatic rifles and a machine-gun, a third hurled a Russian-made grenade. It failed to explode but in the final burst of gunfire two of Mugabe's nephews were injured. Everyone blamed everyone else. Muzorewa said it was the work of rebel elements in Mugabe's own party, the police in Salisbury hinted that it was Nkomo's men. Mugabe, leaving London that night for Africa, pointed the finger at the Rhodesian Security forces. The governor could only reflect that, 'it was shocking ... and must be stopped'.

Still, the British were consoled by the remarkable success of the ceasefire over Christmas and the New Year. Privately men like John Acland, the blunt but admirable commander of the Commonwealth monitoring force, had feared for his men as they were sent out in small groups of 15–20 men to wait for the guerrillas to come into the assembly camps. They were walking into the unknown, armed with hand weapons and c-rations but little else. When just a few hundred reported in the first few days, the men from the Royal Marines, the Irish Guards, the Kenyan Rifles and the New Zealand Infantry appeared not only badly exposed by downright foolhardy. In many camps, they knew they were surrounded by the guerrillas who, suspicious to the last, were 'sniffing them out' before coming in. That it worked said much for the discipline in both guerrilla armies, a lot more for the nerve and patience of Acland and his men. Mugabe's general, Rex Nhongo, and Nkomo's commander, Dumiso Debengwa, urged Acland and Soames to extend the deadline for the guerrillas to report beyond the one agreed at Lancaster House – midnight on Friday, 4 January. Acland would have none of it. 'If we don't get the buggers in now, we never will,' he said. Soames agreed, and the gamble worked. That night, and the following morning, thousands came in, the camps doubled in size within 24 hours. Everyone at Government House breathed a collective sigh of relief. The first hurdle had been cleared. The one that remained was much bigger. To ensure free and fair

179

elections Soames had to rid the country of intimidation, by all parties, as best he could.

In his own mind, he had already made a crucial decision. He could ban candidates, parties, even declare the ballot null and void if he wanted to. But Soames didn't want to. His main weapon, he decided, would be the power of persuasion.

Just as principle had led Carrington to Lancaster House, so it made Soames determined to bring all the parties to election day. The governor, being a horseracing fan, had his own metaphor for his strategy.

'In this particular race,' he told his staff, 'all the horses are going to get to the starting-line come what may. We may have to pull a jockey or two out, even hold an enquiry. But they are all going to start.'

Acland may have been delighted with the final outcome of the ceasefire, but by mid-January he was getting the kind of intelligence reports that told another story. Between 22 December and 6 January, more than 3,000 men of Mugabe's army Zanla had infiltrated from Mozambique into Eastern Rhodesia (so breaking the Lancaster House agreement, which prohibited cross-border movements). Some had gone to the camps, many had not. And, more disturbingly for Government House, they had stored their arms in caches all along the border.

Those who had not gone into the camps, well over 2000, were apparently under orders from Rex Nhongo not to do so. The evidence came from 300 Zanla guerrillas captured by the Rhodesians after the ceasefire deadline. Interrogated by British police advisers, they said Nhongo had given them orders personally to stay away from the camps. Nhongo, they said, had also told them that any subsequent counter-order should be ignored if it appeared to have been made under duress. Not surprisingly, when Nhongo broadcast appeals for them to come in at the governor's insistence, they didn't. This meant that throughout the Eastern Highlands – from Centenary in the north to Chiredzi in the south – there were hundreds of guerrillas still at large, capable of making a mockery of 'free and fair elections'.

At once the reports started coming into the Election Commission. By the time Mugabe got home, a team of eight British election supervisors were putting the finishing touches to an interim report on the progress of the campaign. Their verdict was frightening. More than half the people of Rhodesia were being intimidated by Mugabe's guerrillas and supporters, they said. Conditions for 'fair and free' elections did not exist in five of the eight electoral districts in the country.

Contrary to the claims of Mugabe, the supervisors found little proof of intimidation by Rhodesian security force auxiliaries – the army of about 23,000 created by Muzorewa from the guerrilla who had taken advantage of his amnesty campaign in 1978 and 1979, and the young unemployed.

Only in Victoria province did the supervisors report that the auxiliaries had used 'armed electioneering tactics' to encourage peasants to attend a Muzorewa rally.

It was from Victoria province that the worst evidence had come – and, more damagingly for Mugabe, it had come from his old ally Joshua Nkomo. Nkomo told the governor that three of his workers, a candidate called Francis Makombe and two helpers, were putting up posters in Chibi tribal trust land near Fort Victoria when they were abducted by two gunmen who identified themselves as Zanla 'fighters'. The three of them were marched off to nearby villages, the peasants assembled and ordered to ignore Nkomo's party. The gunmen, Nkomo said, then told the crowd that Mugabe's party had equipment to detect how people voted. Anyone who voted for any candiate other than Mugabe's would have their heads cut off.

The two helpers were beaten, the candidate was last seen with burning coal being stuffed down his throat.

'The word intimidation is mild,' Nkomo said. 'People are being terrorised. It is terror. There is fear in people's eyes.' It was, of course, by no means as one-sided as the interim report suggested.

A visitor to the squatters' camp in the Salisbury township of Harare, where there was little intimidation, could find any number of victims of the Bishop's auxiliaries. A young trader called John Sekere, for example. On 27 January, he was at Zimbabwe grounds to welcome home Mugabe. He went home to Goromozi district, about 30 miles east of Salisbury, with his car loaded with Zanu (PF) posters. He promptly started pasting them everywhere in his village. The auxiliaries, from a unit of Pfumu Revanhu ('spear of the people'), were quickly alerted. Sekere fled but they found his nephew at his shanty, and shot him dead. The hut was burned down. Or Patricia and Irene, both mothers of large families, also from Goromozi. Early one morning in February, they said, the auxiliaries arrived in their village, fired shots over the heads of the peasants and then started systematically beating everyone they found. The reason? They said Zenla guerrillas had been in the village the day before. Bishop Muzorewa, challenged about instances like these, said the people had been 'brainwashed into telling lies'. The fact remains that all these 'victims' were taken back to their homes and their fellow villagers, totally unprepared for journalists, supported the allegations.

Still, *most* of the evidence coming into Government House pointed to Mugabe's men being responsible for *most* of the intimidation. It meant that by the time he returned, Lord Soames knew that some kind of showdown was not only inevitable, it was imperative. And one or two of Soames aides, in their gloomier moments, were admitting that perhaps 'one jockey and one horse might not make it to the starting-line.'

For about 30,000 pounds, the Mugabes had bought a house in the predominantly white suburb of Mount

Pleasant. Number 27, Quorn Avenue, a leafy road of large houses, big cars and manicured dogs. It had been the home of a wealthy white family prominent in the motor car and horse-racing circles. The only remarkable thing about the house was that it didn't have a swimming pool.

The Mugabes moved in on 1 February. A huge stone wall had been built at the bottom of the two acres of lawn, and an iron gate put up. A white policeman was stationed at the gate, Mugabe's own guards came out to check any visitors. The whites out walking their dogs were told to keep away from the house, on the other side of the road. In the first few days, they replied by hooting long and hard on their car horns every time they passed by.

Mugabe was about to move in when he received the call he'd been expecting.

'Hallo, Mr Mugabe, it's the governor's office here. Lord Soames would like to see you. 10 o'clock, OK?'

Mugabe is a fastidious time-keeper. A few weeks later, he was literally one minute late for a meeting with Soames. Bounding up the steps, he said: 'Sorry, we're running on African time today.'

He drove to Government House at a furious speed, determined not to be late. When they pulled into the grounds, six bodyguards leaped out ahead of him all armed with machine-guns. One of the governor's aides came out to greet him and found himself looking at the barrels of several guns. He stood on the steps with his arms outstretched and told Mugabe they could not come in.

Mugabe was a little surprised but he turned to his guards and said: 'No, no, it's alright. You wait out here.'

Soames and Mugabe had never met before. In the main reception room adjoining the governor's office, they shook hands. By nature Soames is a warm, affectionate man, and in the few meetings he'd already had with

Nkomo they'd taken to putting their arms around each other. The opening meeting with Mugabe was decidedly more frosty. Nkomo and Muzorewa had simply come with their advisers. Mugabe was wholly more professional.

Mugabe had his chef de cabinet, Emmerson Munanggwa, one of the first five Zanla guerrillas to train in China and a qualified lawyer. Maurice Nyagumbo, an old-style nationalist who had only been released from prison in November and had since seen Soames regularly on Mugabe's behalf. And, lastly, Miss Otil, a quiet, diligent note-taker who made sure that not just the governor would have a precise record of what was said.

Soames began by saying that he hoped Mugabe did not feel too aggrieved about the delay in coming back.

'Indeed, I do,' answered Mugabe. 'And that's not all ... the ceasefire has been broken repeatedly by the security forces and the auxiliaries ... there are South African units in many places ... this is not what I had expected.'

Soames patiently heard him out, then replied with the charge of intimidation against Zanla units. Mugabe did not concede that some of his men had stayed out of the camps deliberately, he did admit there had been problems in getting the message through to his forces.

'The death of Tongogara caused great confusion,' he said. After 90 minutes that were 'cordial', but really not too friendly, Lord Soames had the last word.

'This country has got to get a clean bill of health,' the governor said. 'I look to you.'

Three days later, 15 black civilians were killed and more than 20 injured when a bus was ambushed about 100 miles east of Salisbury on the road to Umtali. The rockets and small arms used suggested Zanla was responsible. A peace that had always been fragile, said one of General Walls' aides, was not just cracking at the seams, it was falling apart.

Under his emergency powers, the governor could already ban Mugabe's party from the election. Now he issued an ordinance that enabled him to restrict party meetings, suspend a candidate from campaigning and disqualify a party in any one district.

On Saturday, 10 February Enos Nkala, a hard-liner who had spent 15 years in detention and was now Mugabe's leading candidate in Matebeleland, told a rally there that the war would resume if Mugabe did not win the election. He had already been quoted as saying that 'the governor can go hang'.

That, said Soames, was incitement. Government House announced on the Sunday that Nkala, a one-time clerk who had become the party's treasurer, was banned from campaigning.

That Sunday Mugabe was in Fort Victoria. It was only the second major rally of his campaign. The turn-out was healthy enough, about 25,000, in the township of Muchoke. They heard Mugabe's most bitter attack to date on the governor. He would, he said, order his men to leave the assembly camps if Lord Soames attempted to ban his party (not just individuals like Nkala) from contesting the election in any region.

'If Lord Soames should use his new powers to ban Zanu (PF) then Zanu (PF) will consider itself absolved from the Lancaster House agreement. We will not continue to keep our forces in the assembly camps if we are banned,' Mugabe said.

Mugabe's motorcade had been held up by the crowds and was well behind schedule when it left for the local airstrip to meet the plane taking him back to Salisbury. As the convoy turned into the access road leading to the airstrip, it happened.

A huge bomb exploded underneath the motorcade.

Mugabe was shaken, badly, but not hurt. Five guards in the car behind him were injured. It was the narrowest of escapes.

Everything about the attack suggested a sophistication beyond the reach of the ordinary. About 90 pounds of TNT had been used. Part of it had been detonated electrically by someone standing in long grass about 100 yards from the road. (Some witnesses said that gunmen followed up the explosion by opening fire on Mugabe's cars. The claim was never substantiated.) There was also a mine placed in a culvert under the road. It did not go off. The Rhodesian bomb experts who detonated it later remarked that its construction showed a great deal of expertise. The following day Mugabe, back at his home in Salisbury, went on the offensive against the governor.

'It was obviously the work of the Rhodesian security forces whom the governor has chosen to deploy,' he told a press conference in his back garden. 'Its just one of the many strategies which have been worked out by the British, the South Africans and the Rhodesians to prevent my party participating in the elections.'

Taking treatment like this, he said, made him look like a traitor to his men in the camps.

'I won't continue to insist on my forces remaining in assembly points if the people continue to be exposed to the Rhodesian Forces and the auxiliaries. If Lord Soames doesn't check them ... we will restart the war.'

It was the lowest point of the whole peace process. And yet the following day Mugabe was to change the course of it all with a display of defiance, honesty and reason that astounded everyone at Government House.

Soames called Mugabe to Government House for six o'clock in the evening. Mugabe arrived with his two most senior men on the Central Committee – Simon Muzenda, his deputy, and Edgar Tekere, a militant who had held out longer than most against the Lancaster House agreement. Mugabe did not give Lord Soames much of a chance. Polite but firm, he launched into a bitter attack against the way the ceasefire was being handled. It was not just the Fort Victoria attack, now there was evidence

186

that the Rhodesian Air Force had bombed two villages in the north-east on the Mozambique border. Mugabe said he would take the governor there if he liked. Soames declined saying it would not be necessary. The Air Force had not bombed anyone. The governor said the monitors checked every plane movement, even counting the number of bombs they had in store after every sortie, however routine. The governor's staff suspected Mugabe's apparent willingness to believe almost anything his supporters told him. The 'bombing' claim was preposterous, they said. Another was the 'disappearance' of 200 ballot papers, reported in the Rhodesian press. Mugabe claimed that two million had gone missing.

Lord Soames made it clear that he would take action unless Mugabe stopped intimidation by his supporters in certain areas – notably Manicaland, along the border with Mozambique. Nkomo, Muzorewa and all the other parties said they simply could not campaign there for fear of reprisals, Lord Soames declared.

Mugabe seized on this at once.

'Look, Lord Soames,' he said. 'I'm not new to this game, you know. That's my part of the country, Manicaland, that's mine. The fact that Nkomo can't campaign there is down to the fact that I control it, I've had a cell system there for five years. It is surprising that people don't turn out there for Nkomo? Would I go to Nkomo country (Matebeleland) and expect to raise a crowd there? Of course, I wouldn't.'

Soames, quickly gathering his thoughts, repeated his warning of a few days earlier.

'I still look to you, Mr Mugabe, to stop the intimidation. I want all candidates and all parties to hold free meetings wherever they are,' the governor said.

Government House's approach to Mugabe after that assault on the ethics of electioneering was never the same. To say that they treated him with a lot more respect is an understatement. They knew that there was no answer to his claim to control huge areas of the country. The only recourse would have been to outlaw him from the elections – and that, they all knew, would only unleash a new war.

There was, however, one other alternative, and over the weeks it had become a favourite talking-point in white, business and British circles in Salisbury, including those at Government House.

On the likely assumption that Mugabe would win a simple majority of seats (35–40 was the most popular projection at this stage), but not a clear one (50 +), did there exist a coalition of forces that would exclude him? An anti-Mugabe coalition looked good on paper to the whites, to the business community, even to some at Government House (not Lord Soames, it must be said). It was particularly appealing if it included Joshua Nkomo. With him on board, probably as prime minister in a coalition including Muzarewa and the whites, the new Zimbabwe would get the backing of at least two Front Line States, Zambia and Botswana. Add to them South Africa, the EEC, Nato and the Soviet Union (Nkomo's arms supplier, after all) and it made sense. At least it would make sense to many Western governments and international business.

It was no secret that some senior figures at Government House did more than just nurture the idea, they positively encouraged it. Nkomo himself did nothing to discourage them. He would prefer to form a coalition with Mugabe. But he was really leaving all options open.

Ironically, Mugabe did try to go to Nkomo country to campaign. On 17 February, he was due to appear at the Barbourfields football stadium in Bulawayo. Two weeks before Nkomo had drawn a huge crowd there, estimated at 200,000. About 50,000 waited for Mugabe, which made nonsense of his claim that he could not expect to raise a crowd in the part of the country. He did not show; there had been death threats against him.

That same Sunday, Combined Operations Headquarters in Salisbury put out an unprecedented communiqué explaining a spate of bomb attacks in the capital the previous Thursday night. The security forces tried to hide their embarrassment, but they could not conceal the strongest evidence of a campaign of 'dirty tricks' aimed at Mugabe and his party. The bare facts of the case were that two churches in the city centre were severely damaged by bombs. The blast from one of them also caused severe damage to the Monomotapa Hotel in the city centre, where several British officials, including John Boynton, were staying. No one was seriously hurt.

The same night an explosion occurred near a church in the black township of Harare. To be precise, it occurred in the back of the car of the bombers, and it killed them both instantly. Both were black.

At once the police let it be known that they had 'concluded' that it was a campaign of terrorism against Christian churches. Bishop Muzorewa and the Rhodesian Front said it could only have been the work of Marxists. After all, had not Mugabe once said that all Christian holidays would be banned under him? And that the State religion would be his own atheism? He had also said in his manifesto that there would be religious freedom.

The following day another unexploded bomb was found at the side of the Roman Catholic cathedral in Salisbury. On it were written pro-Mugabe slogans, admittedly in bad Shona. But they were in Shona which, as the police noted immediately, was the language of the regions which most strongly supported Mugabe.

It all pointed to Marxists. Or did it?

Some Mugabe supporters had got to the bombed-out car in Harare before the police and found the vehicle's registration certificate.

The owners of the car were members of the Selous

189

Scouts, the crack Rhodesian army unit which had master-minded the raids into Zambia and Mozambique during the war.

That Sunday Combined Operations made a poor job of explaining it all. The two dead men were named, Lieutenant Edward Piringondo and Corporal Morgan Moyo, from which unit no one was supposed to know.

The communiqué said: 'It has been established that about 55 minutes before the explosion at Harare, the two men had made a telephone report to their duty officer. They had information about the presence of two Zanla terrorists. The men were instructed to follow up their information and to report back when possible.'

The communiqué did not explain how two soldiers came to be sitting in a car with a bomb in the back; why they had taken it upon themselves to do police work; even what two soldiers were doing on duty in a township when they should have been in barracks under the cease-fire.

Not for nothing, said one of Mugabe's spokesmen that night, were the Selous Scouts trained to disguise them-selves as guerrillas when the occasion called for it.

A week later on the final weekend of the campaign, the left-wing newspaper *Moto* appeared on the streets from its publishing house in the Midlands town of Gwelo. Or, to put the question once more, did it?

Moto had not long been back in publication; its support for the Patriotic Front had seen it banned for years under Smith and Muzorewa.

The dateline on this edition, saying 'Saturday, 12 February 1980,' did not necessarily give it away. Everything else purported to be the real thing. The banner was the same, the typesetting identical to *Moto*'s, it even had stories favourable to the Front. Its front-page splash was anything but. It was headlined 'Robert Mugabe – profile of the man.'

It was a savage indictment of Mugabe, crediting him

with everything from an 'Oedipus complex' to a lust for power that would stop at nothing. Every myth surrounding his name was exploited.

'Who is Robert Mugabe?' it began. 'Is he an enlightened progressive Christian leader of a people seeking their destiny or is he a ruthless, power-hungry Marxist heathen?'

It ended: 'One cannot escape the conclusion that he is a psychopath suffering from paranoia – in layman's terms the man can be considered mentally ill.'

At 2 a.m. the morning after the fake issue of *Moto* was circulated, the Mambo printing press which normally published the newspaper was blown up. No doubt it was designed to be seen as a reprisal by Mugabe's supporters for the scurrilous attack. But again the bombers were the victims: they died in the explosion too. And the charred remains suggested they were not Mugabe's saboteurs. Because one of them was white.

Under 'free and fair elections' that final weekend of the campaign would have seen the candidates out on the hustings, driving home their message to the voters. At least that was the design of Lancaster House.

Instead, Mugabe was at home in Quorn Avenue. A rally he had planned in Umtali was cancelled when police found rockets and mortars hidden just a few hundred yards from the showground where it should have been held.

Nkomo was in Gwelo, the town picking up the pieces after the bombing at the Mambo presses the night before. Nkomo had fought a skilful, clever campaign, but he had rarely got outside his native Matebeleland to prove it. On this, the last real campaign day, he was to show what might have been. It was not a fighting speech, more an impassioned statement of his credentials as the father of Rhodesian nationalism, depicting himself as the only man under whom everyone could unite.

Bishop Muzorewa was in Salisbury, leading the final

jamboree of a campaign that was arguably the most expensive ever waged in Africa. It had cost his Rhodesian and South African backers millions of dollars and this was the culmination of it all. A four-day rally in Zimbabwe grounds, from Thursday to Sunday, with free shelter, free food, free paper hats.

By now several hundred observers from all over the world, sent by governments, political parties, even research institutes, were in Salisbury to witness the election. Those who attended the Bishop's rally learned their first lesson. 'I can't believe it,' said one Dutch observer. 'This man is buying votes, with no shame.'

General Walls spent that final weekend of the campaign in Maputo, Mozambique. After his customary game of tennis on Saturday morning he and Ken Flower, the head of Rhodesia's central intelligence, flew out in secret on one of the most dramatic missions of the entire Rhodesia story. It was very much at the behest of Government House, John Acland in particular.

The official version was that General Walls and Mr Flower met ministers of the Mozambican Government to discuss the post-election period in Rhodesia. In fact, they went specifically to get President Machel's assurance that he would accept the result of the poll, whatever its imperfections and whatever the outcome. In return, they gave Machel's ministers a guarantee that there would be no military coup if Mugabe won.

When Walls came home on Sunday night, he had a mass of paper work to get through. The following morning, just 48 hours before the elections were due to start, about 600 men of Nkomo's army Zipra were to report in a camp at Essexvale near Bulawayo for training with Rhodesian units. It had long been Nkomo's dream to set up a joint army of guerrillas and Rhodesian regulars, one-time enemies in the same force. It would be a symbol of the new order in Rhodesia, said Nkomo. It also held a possible solution for one of Government House's main worries – what to do with the guerrillas once the election was over. Reading the brief written for him, Walls thought it was a positive step, but he was not sure whether it would solve the problem. And, anyway, he had other things on his mind. A coup was not out of the question. Walls would not lead it – he was being honest when he said that he would serve if asked whatever government came to power – but he knew that his 'middle management' of white officers might ask him to sanction it. At this stage, Walls simply did not know how he would react to that.

His prime sentiment, in the run-up to the election, was frustration – frustration with the way, in his view, Muzorewa had been outwitted at Lancaster House and outfought in the election. He sensed Mugabe would win, by what margin he could not know, and that is why he had agreed to go to Mozambique. But that did not mean he liked it. He was to vent his frustration by writing to Mrs Thatcher asking that she declare the result null and void. She never replied.

That Sunday, Lord Soames made his final review of the situation. The question in front of him was whether or not to ban polling in areas where intimidation was rife. His staff had maps, showing that in more than a quarter of the country no parties other than Mugabe's had been able to campaign. The latest tally from the ceasefire commission showed that the vast majority of the 207 breaches reported had been attributed to Mugabe's army. The number of contacts between the Rhodesian forces and 'bandits' (guerrillas who had not gone into the assembly camps) was now running at nine or ten a day, twice the level of a few weeks earlier and mainly in the Eastern Highlands, Mugabe country. It was, in the view of some British advisers, a systematic and calculated campaign of violence and intimidation by Zanu (PF).

'You have a situation,' explained one of those advisers, 'where eight black parties are trying to carry out a political campaign and one is conducting a paramilitary exercise.'

By western standards, yes, there had been an intolerable degree of intimidation and it was not just Mugabe's party. But in the context of Rhodesia, of a country at war for seven years?

Soames decided, in his own mind at least, on the lesser of two evils. He would let the election go ahead, whatever the doubts about its integrity, rather than ban polling and so provoke a probable civil war.

Lady Soames' good work and innate political skill should not be overlooked in assessing her husband's role. Not only did she help build relations with all the party leaders, she was also a tireless worker on behalf of charities handling orphans and refugees. That was to impress Sally Mugabe, who wrote to Elizabeth Walston in May: 'Lady Soames has great feelings for the suffering children. She did some good work. I only wish she could have stayed longer.'

That afternoon the governor and his wife Mary attended an inter-denominational service at the Salisbury showground. Along with about 500 others, mostly whites, they prayed for peace whatever the outcome of the election.

By Monday morning Sir John Boynton and his election staff were ready to go. It was a massive operation; they had been working at the logistics non-stop ever since December. Not least of Boynton's problems was that he did not know just how many people could or would vote.

The black population was thought to number about seven million. Less than three million were believed to be entitled to vote (all adults, over 18, including foreigners if they had lived in the country for more than two years). There was no electoral register, indeed no reliable census. To prevent anyone voting more than once, a simple chemical precaution would be used. The voter would, on arrival at a polling station, have his hands examined by

194

a scanning machine. If the machine did not respond, he would be given a ballot paper and his hands would be dipped into a colourless chemical which reflected ultra-violet light. If he or she attempted to vote a second time, the scanner would react to the chemical. The chemical was, of course, designed to leave traces for more than the three days of polling.

There were 657 polling stations and nearly half of them were mobile, vans travelling round the rural areas and the remote tribal trustlands. At such there would be a British policeman, something of an anachronism it seemed, but in fact a figure of authority that many Africans did recognise. It was his job to make sure only the voters entered the stations and that no one started singing, chanting or shouting party slogans within a 100 yards of the polling booth. At the end of the day the policeman would make sure the boxes were sealed, if necessary he would sleep with them to make sure they were not tampered with.

Early on Tuesday morning the great airlift started. Millions of ballot papers, thousands of ballot boxes, hundreds of those scanners flown from Salisbury to those stations throughout the country. The planes had come from Britain, America, Canada. The trucks were Rhodesian, each one escorted by the security forces in mine-protected vehicles. No one was taking chances, least of all General Walls. Come that Tuesday morning, every available soldier and policeman was on duty. Leave had been cancelled weeks before, now Walls had called up almost every reserve, young and old. It gave him 60,000 men for a massive, highly visible display of security. In Salisbury, roadblocks were put on every way into the city, manned by police and backed by army units, some of them with decidedly heavy artillery at their disposal. Truckloads of policemen and soldiers patrolled the town-ships and infantry units guarded key installations like the radio and television station and the ministries. There was even a tank outside the entrance to Salisbury University, where officers of Zanla and Zipra had been staying since coming home in December.

Out on the country thousands of territorials, backed up by the Auxilaries, were deployed at every community numbering more than a few dozen. Armoured cars with cannon roamed through the tribal trustlands, stopping at every kraal and village to let everyone know they were in charge.

Combined Operations reported at 4 p.m. that it had been a quiet day, no contacts between the security forces and the 'bandits'.

At 3.30 Mugabe arrived at Government House with Munanggwa, Nyagumbo, and Miss Otil. The governor's private secretary met them at the door.

'The governor would like to see you alone,' he told Mugabe.

'Alone?' asked Mugabe. 'What ... you mean without my secretary?'

'No ... alone.'

'I suppose you'll be there,' said Mugabe.

'No, just you and Lord Soames.'

Mugabe went into the reception room, where the governor was waiting for him. He led him into his office and shut the door.

Soames began by asking why Mugabe was delaying in getting his men into the camp where Nkomo's units were training with the Rhodesians. Mugabe denied that he had been 'dragging his feet', as he put it: he wanted to start integrating the armies as soon as possible and he would go to see John Acland about it as soon as he had finished talking to the governor.

Changing subjects quickly, Mugabe said that the police behaviour in the past few days had been 'scandalous'. About 5000 of his supporters had been detained in the previous week, he claimed. Lord Soames disregarded that, but since Mugabe had brought up allegations of intimidation, what about the campaign of Zanu (PF)? 'I will not forget it,' the governor told him. 'You know just what a big factor intimidation, by your people, has been in this election.'

Mugabe did not answer the charge.

Nevertheless, said Lord Soames, he would not be using his powers to ban polling anywhere or disenfranchise voters in any part of the country.

'I think its in the best interests of Rhodesia that all parties start this election,' he said.

Mugabe may have been delighted, but he did not let it show. The formalities over, the governor asked what his plans were, how he saw the future.

Mugabe paused for a second, then explained. There would be no instant, radical change, no sweeping national-isation of either industry or land, and no hounding of the whites. He wanted the whites to stay, he said, without them the economy could be wrecked. He also wanted Walls to stay on, to ease the fears of the whites and build up a disciplined military from his own forces and those of the Patriotic Front.

Then he turned to independence.

'When I'm prime minister,' he said, 'independence ought not to come too quickly. We need time, Lord Soames ... and I would like you to stay on for as long as possible.'

The governor thanked him for that. It would be con-sidered, he said. After an hour, Mugabe went off to see Acland about the integration of the armies.

'Goodbye, Robert,' said Soames pointedly as he left. The two had not been on first-name terms till now. 'Goodbye, Lord Soames,' replied Mugabe.

It had been a crucial meeting, both men looked back on it as the 'turning-point' in the relationship. It was significant for a number of reasons. Not least the fact that neither had doubted who was going to be prime minister.

Half an hour later Mugabe walked to his car with the governor's secretary. They talked about the poll and the plans for it. As he shook hands, Mugabe said: 'I'm going to win 56 seats.'

That night, as Mugabe and all the other party leaders were making their final appeals to the nation with recorded messages on radio and television, a silver Mercedes pulled up at the house in Quron Avenue. It was waved through the minute Mugabe's guards saw who it was.

General Walls had come at Mugabe's request. Walls told him there would be no coup *if* he won. Mugabe asked him to stay on as commander of the armed forces *when* he did.

In some places, notably the townships of the major cities, they started queuing in the middle of the night. By five in the morning, the line at the main polling station in Harare was half a mile long. There were the occasional shouts of a party slogan, some of Mugabe's supporters even pranced up and down the line flapping their elbows and imitating the shrill of the cockerel, the party symbol. By dawn, loudspeaker vans were out in the towns reminding people to vote.

At seven o'clock that morning, the stations opened. In the cities, there was a rush to vote before work started, in the rural areas it was more leisurely (many there would have to wait until the mobile booth came round). But from the first few hours it was clear the turn-out would be massive.

There were a few hiccups. The woman in Bulawayo, for example, who realised she had put her cross against the wrong party, crumpled her paper up and stuffed it into her brassiere before going to the back of the line to try again. She was arrested, taken before a magistrate and cautioned.

Or the taxi driver, again in Bulawayo, who thought he was quite within his rights to ferry people to the polling station in a car literally covered with Nkomo posters.

To the genuine surprise of the election supervisors, all the major parties did take up the invitation to send agents to watch polling in the areas where intimidation had been worst. On election day at least, the poll was to affect to the standards of freedom and fairness. At Chiredzi in the south-east, for example, small groups of agents for Muzorewa, Nkomo and Sithole gathered (some of them breaking the rules by putting up posters) outside the main polling station in the town. Yet none of them had campaigned there for fear of reprisals from Zanu (PF).

Here, deep in the heart of Mugabe country where war had been a way of life for years, his people could afford benign tolerance to the opposition.

'I tell my supporters to leave them alone,' said Mugabe's main candidate in Chiredzi, Nelson Mawema. 'Let them do what they like. Because they have no chance here, no chance at all.'

By mid-afternoon on that first day, nearly a million people had voted. There was little intimidation, said observers. Rather a mood of excitement and good humour.

Soames went to watch the polling in Harare, then returned to Government House to another decision. He was already looking ahead of the elections, to the following Tuesday, 4 March, when the result would be announced.

The British had about 300 monitors out in the guerrilla assembly camps, surrounded by thousands of armed men whose reaction to the result, whichever way it went, was impossible to predict.

John Acland was insistent that the majority should be pulled out before then, and that the Rhodesians should move in, albeit in small numbers. A few monitors, all volunteers, should stay behind to keep the peace if necessary.

Acland had a formidable reputation with all his men. Like most soldiers, they distrusted politicians but they trusted Acland. One of the factors crucial in keeping up morale and nerve in the early days had been the common soldier's reasoning that, if things were going wrong, Acland would get them out. Now Acland wanted them out, he saw no point at all in having them all at risk if the result went against the leader of the guerrillas they had charge of.

Walls was persuaded to move in small units of his army, quietly, discreetly on the day before the result. Six monitors, most of whom had built up a good relationship with the guerrillas, would stay with them for the day of the result, with plans well laid for evacuation if necessary. In one of the largest Zanla camps the British major was to brief journalists on those plans the night before the result. 'If it goes wrong,' he said, 'we all beat it up the hillside, where we've got enough mortars to hold them off for a couple of hours. By then the choppers [helicopters] will be in.'

Eddison Zvobgo explained that Mugabe wanted to heal the breach between Nyerere and Machel over the validity of the poll. Just two days before Nyerere had claimed the British would rig the election in favour of Muzorewa. Machel had argued that the poll would be valid, whatever the outcome. The fact was that Machel had Fernando Honwana in Salisbury to brief him, Nyerere had no one.

Acland was infuriated. Mugabe had no more important task than telling his men to behave, he said. The governor's staff shared his anger, particularly when they checked with Machel in Maputo and found that the trip was not at the president's request, but Mugabe's initiative.

200

Once again, Mugabe was mistrusted and suspected by some of the most senior figures at Government House.

Come the weekend, Nkomo toured his camps with Acland spelling out the orders clearly. Instead of Mugabe, Simon Muzenda visited the Zanla camps – and there the atmosphere was decidedly tense.

The last to vote were the guerrillas in the camps. On Friday night, the polls closed, the ballot boxes were flown back to Salisbury. On Saturday morning the count began.

Everyone now waited, Lord Soames, John Acland, Joshua Nkomo, Bishop Muzorewa. Everyone, it seemed, apart from Mugabe. He flew in from Tanzania on Sunday and told the press: 'The governor is duty-bound to choose me to form a government, It is inevitable, whether we have an overall majority or not.'

It started as informed speculation, leaks from the party agents and election commissioners who had seen the ballots being counted. By four o'clock on the Monday afternoon, 17 hours before the declaration, it was hard news for the 800-odd journalists in Salisbury.

Mugabe had won. And won so convincingly that a coalition would not be necessary.

In Salisbury alone, the agents had seen a quarter of a million votes for Mugabe, just 50,000 for Muzorewa, half that for Nkomo. Mugabe had swept the board in Manicaland, Victoria province, even the midlands where Nkomo had hoped to do well.

Zvobgo, as always, provided the quotes for the press. Arriving at the press centre in the Meikles hotel in the centre of Salisbury, he predicted 60 seats for Mugabe.

'It is no longer a question of whether we will win but only by what margin ... that should be no surprise to anybody.'

He could even afford magnanimity towards Nkomo.

'We want him to join us,' Zvobgo said. 'Mr Nkomo

has contributed a great deal to national unity, he has suffered, and he is everybody's grandfather.'

As Zvobgo was doing the first lap of honour, the governor's office was telephoning both General Walls and Mugabe. The governor wanted them to join him in a nationwide broadcast that night, to appeal for calm on the morrow.

Soames went first. 'This is a solemn hour for Zimbabwe. There must be no violent action or reaction of any kind ... my purpose is to bring about an orderly transfer of power to a stable government.'

Walls followed. 'I appeal to you all for calm, peace, and no hatred or bitterness ... but anybody who gets out of line will be dealt with effectively and swiftly, and, I may say, with quite a lot of enthusiasm.'

Mugabe was last. 'Let us join together, let us show respect for the winners and the losers.'

It could have been an anti-climax – he knew, after all, that he had won – but Mugabe was determined to savour every minute of it. At nine o'clock the following morning he, Sally and dozens of their helpers, comrades like Muzenda, Nkala, Tekere, were waiting in front of the television set in Quorn Avenue. Some of the girls, the girls who had been in Maputo, Geneva, London, could not bear to watch. Sally made them sit down.

On the stroke of 9 a.m., John Boynton began to read the roll call of the parties. Cheers for Nkomo's 20 seats. Jeers for Muzorewa's 3. Zanu (PF) was right at the end.

The Mugabe household only heard '57'. The rest was drowned out in cheers. Sally hugged everyone in sight, Mugabe himself stood up motionless for a few seconds, numbed it seemed by the size of victory.

'My heart went bang, bang, bang,' he said as he beat his chest with his fist.

The phone rang. It was Soames' secretary. '10 o'clock, OK?'

Sally went outside to join the few dozen who had gathered in Quorn Avenue to hear the news on the radio. When Mugabe left for Government House, she was dancing in the street.

At assembly camp Foxtrot, about 200 miles south-east of Salisbury, the black and white Rhodesian soldiers stood to attention on their tiny ad hoc parade ground, surrounded by the tents in which they had just spent their first night. They had arrived at dusk the evening before and made camp about 500 yards from the main body of guerrillas. Their commanding officer told them not to be nervous, but they were.

About half of the 6000 Zanla troops in the camp marched to the huge training compound exactly 10 minutes before the declaration. 'At ease,' said their commander, promptly pulling out his radio and playing with the aerial to get decent reception. Dozens of his men, their Kalishnikov rifles on their shoulders, crowded round. Nkomo's patriotic front, Muzorewa's UANC, Sithole's Zanu.

Then the result ... and pandemonium. It took the commander 10 minutes to calm them down.

'Viva President Mugabe,' he shouted.

'Viva,' came the deafening reply.

Major Tim Purdon, of the Irish guards, watched from the sidelines. 'Who would have thought...?' he said.

In the major cities – Salisbury, Bulawayo, Umtali – some white children had been sent to school with bags already packed in case the rumours of a Mugabe victory were proved correct at nine o'clock. Husbands did phone wives and tell them to get ready to go to South Africa. Resignations poured in, to the banks, to the mining companies, to the ministries. Estate agents had been busy for years with the white exodus. That morning they put hundreds of houses on the market.

Despite all the excitement, Mugabe was on time at Government House. It would have been improper for the governor to congratulate him. He thought that Mrs Thatcher would do it in the House of Commons. But the mood of the Conservative was as gloomy as that of the whites and she pointedly refrained from any public congratulations that day. One of her MPs said: 'We were told peace was preferable to the bullet. We weren't told that the effect would be the same.' Lord Soames simply shook Mugabe's hand and beckoned him into his room. Mugabe had brought Enos Nkala, the candidate Soames had banned.

'I don't think you know Mr Nkala,' said Mugabe.

'Ah, yes, Mr Nkala,' said the governor. 'I don't think I've heard you making many speeches lately.'

The next minister of Zimbabwe was not amused.

He had not been elected in Matebeleland and he said so. 'You cost me my seat,' he told Lord Soames.

Mugabe smiled, nervously. He and the governor retired alone. The winner was full of praise for the governor. Lord Soames had been magnificent, he said. Mugabe had not expected him to allow the elections to go ahead 'unhindered' and the fact that he had said much for his courage.

'We must join hands and work together, all of us,' Mugabe said.

Lord Soames told him how important it was for him to create just that impression when he spoke to the nation later. In the next 45 minutes Mugabe and the governor hammered out the draft out of the broadcast, not on paper but in Mugabe's mind.

'Were I in your position,' was how Lord Soames put it to him, 'I would do this...'

At the end of their meeting, Mugabe said: 'Goodbye, Christopher, and thank you.'

The next to arrive was Nkomo, close to tears, clearly very tired and dispirited. One of his first comments silenced, indeed astounded, everyone in the room.

'You give them one man one vote and look what they do with it,' Nkomo said.

He was bitter about Mugabe and the decision to go the polls separately.

'We should have fought the election together ... Robert let me down.'

Lord Soames gave him a stiff drink but Nkomo could not be consoled.

'I'm too old for all this,' he said. 'I will get out of politics.'

The last visitor of the morning was Bishop Muzorewa. When his deputy, Silas Mundawara, began to carp about intimidation, Muzorewa snapped: 'Stop it ... its all over now'.

He told Soames: 'The most important thing is that we don't have persecution of the losers.'

The celebrations in the black townships lasted all day: as did the sense of shock and mourning in the white suburbs and down on the white farms. By eight o'clock that night, however, the nation was united in something: watching or listening to the new prime minister-elect.

A rather stiff white lady introduced him on television as 'Comrade Robert G. Mugabe.' That was the only moment that could have worried anyone.

The 'bloodthirsty Communist terrorist', the man who once said he would execute Ian Smith when he came to power, the man who Ian Smith once accused of 'walking around on cloud nine in camouflage' was articulate, compassionate, thoughtful, above all conciliatory.

'There is no intention on our part to use our majority to victimise the minority. We will ensure there is a place for everyone in this country. We want to ensure a sense of security for both the winners and the losers,' he said.

He spelt out what he wanted – a broadly based coalition to include the whites as well as Nkomo.

Step by step, he allayed all the fears of those for whom his arrival signalled their departure. He spoke to them one by one.

To the business community: there would be no sweeping nationalisation.

To white civil servants: your pensions and your jobs will be guaranteed.

To farmers and house-owners: your rights to your property will be respected.

And to the world at large: Zimbabwe will be tied to no one, it will be strictly non-aligned.

Even to South Africa: we offer peaceful coexistence.

'Let us forgive and forget, let us join hands in a new amity.'

By Wednesday morning, all but a handful of those resignations had been withdrawn. And hundreds of houses were taken off the market.

'Rhodesians,' said Ian Smith, going as far as to call Mugabe practical and sensible, 'have learned to live with a crisis. They will see this one through.'

A week later Mugabe started fulfilling some of those promises. Walls was indeed made supreme commander of the armed forces, Nkomo was given the interior ministry, and two whites were included in his first cabinet.

Both were bold, brave choices. David Smith, a long-time ally of Ian Smith in the Rhodesia Front, was made commerce minister. And Dennis Norman, the president of the white farmers' union, was appointed to the agriculture portfolio. That was the ultimate compromise, the final statement on Mugabe's politics of pragmatism. Land was the reason for his war, to win it for his people had always been the goal. Now he was putting a white into the ministry that would oversee the full utilisation of all the land rather than the instant expropriation of it, from the whites to the peasants.

*

At the end of March, Sally Mugabe sent a postcard to Elizabeth Walston.

She wrote: 'Yes, Elizabeth, my dear, it's victory and peace at last. It's simply beautiful to walk the streets of Salisbury without harassment. Everyone is a human being now.

Does this mean war is good because it brings peace?'

Chapter 8 — Conclusion

At midnight on 17 April 1980, Zimbabwe was reborn, amidst jubilation, at the Rufaro stadium. On the stroke of 12·00 a.m., to a mounting crescendo of noise around the terraces, the last British flag over Africa was hauled down to be replaced by the flag of the new Zimbabwe: stripes of green (for the land), gold (for the minerals), red (for the blood spilled), and black (for the people). There was no national anthem because Mugabe had insisted that they got it right, rather than writing something in haste, and they hadn't.

It had been a strange enough sight at Government House before the independence ceremony: a cocktail party at which old enemies like Peter Walls and Kenneth Kaunda mingled with Prince Charles, Sally Mugabe and Mary Soames. Now, on the podium at Rufaro, an even more unlikely group sealed the transfer of power to the Africans after 89 years of white rule.

There was Mugabe, almost having to pinch himself to believe that it was really happening; the Reverend Canaan Banana, the first president of the new country; Lord Soames, his joy tinged with relief that he had not been the governor of blood chaos; Prince Charles, who had seen many an independence day but never one like this; and Chief Justice Hector Macdonald, resplendent in robes and wig.

'In terms of section 28 of the constitution of Zimbabwe,' he said as he swore in President Banana. Some of those present, remembering the judge from his earlier days, said they almost expected him to add: 'I order you to be hanged by the neck until dead.'

The themes of that heady night in Salisbury were

Mugabe's – reconciliation, reconstruction, forgiveness, and, above all, love,

Speaking of Lord Soames, he said: 'I must admit that I was one of those who originally never trusted him. And yet I have ended up not only implicitly trusting him but also fondly loving him as well.'

And turning to his nation at large, he declared: 'If yesterday I fought you as an enemy, today you have become a friend. If yesterday you hated me, today you cannot avoid the love that binds you to me and me to you.'

All the dignitaries picked up where he had left off. Prince Charles: 'To heal what has been hurt and wounded, to reunite what has been divided, and to reconcile where there has been emnity is the finest foundation on which to rebuild and increase this quality of life in your unique country.'

And the Queen, in a message to Mugabe himself: 'It is a moment for people of all races and all political persuasions to forget the bitterness of the past and to work together to build a better future for their country and for their citizens.'

When Zimbabwe woke up, the newspapers reported singing and dancing throughout the country. They also carried the 'in memoriam' columns.

The parents of one white grieved for their son 'Killed in action one year ago today, 18th April 1979 ... what it meant to lose you no one will ever know. We often wonder why. Was it all for nothing?'

In the months since independence, it's a question many Rhodesians – black and white – have asked of Mugabe.

In the past year the pressures on him have been tremendous – from within his own party, from his own army, from old rivals like Nkomo, from old rivals like Peter Walls.

Mugabe's voice of moderation and conciliation has never faltered but it has been an increasingly difficult

210

position to maintain. Because on almost every major issue he has been forced to try the impossible – please all the people all the time.

The fact remains that after just one, extremely difficult year, Mugabe has already strengthened his own position immeasurably by his own performance so far.

When he came to power, there were three ways Mugabe's rule was threatened, three scenarios, if you like, of how Mugabe could fall:

- Because of a civil war
- Because of a split between himself and Nkomo
- Because of a massive exodus of whites which would destroy his plans for the economy.

Today all the signs are that Mugabe is winning on all three fronts.

Take the guerrilla armies, for example, and the latent threat they have always posed of a civil war. Lancaster House found them homes, in the Assembly camps, during the ceasefire and the election campaign. It never even began to tackle the problem of what to do with them afterwards. For months they have been left there, bored, restless, questioning what they would get out of peace having fought the war. Most wanted to stay in the army but only hundreds, not their thousands, could be integrated into the new national force. Inevitably, violence has followed.

At some camps, like X-ray near the town of Mtoko north-east of Salisbury, they took the law into their own hands, seizing control of the main roads around the town and arbitrarily ambushing civilian and military vehicles. Policemen and farmers in the town have been killed. For months, the Government seemed unable, or reluctant, to find those responsible, even enforce discipline in an around camp.

Mugabe had long since known there would be trouble like this. And, in the eyes of the whites in particular, the

211

action he has taken has only served to exacerbate the situation. In September 1980, he moved about 17,000 guerrillas, most loyal to him but some from Nkomo's army too, into temporary accommodation at Chitungwiza, just 15 miles from the centre of Salisbury. A huge fence was put up around the housing estate where the soldiers were given homes. Guards manned the exit gates and guerrillas were ordered to hand in their weapons when going out. Within days Nkomo's men were fighting Mugabe's units. Only heavy army and police reinforcements prevents open warfare on the doorstep of Salisbury.

Open warfare did break out on the streets of Bulawayo in November when at least 55 people died and more than 200 were wounded in 24 hours of street battles between the two rival armies for control of another of these temporary homes. Mugabe personally ordered in the new national army and their air force to keep the peace.

On the face of it, the battle in Bulawayo was as damaging to Mugabe as anything so far. In reality, it may just be another step towards securing his own self-preservation. His problem with the guerrillas had always been how to disarm them, how to separate them from the Kalishnikov rifles, their grenade launchers and mortars. In these temporary homes at least they could not go out with their weapons. And in the wake of Bulawayo, Mugabe had a perfectly adequate 'political excuse' for ordering the army to strip the guerrilla units of all heavy weapons.

Not for the first time since independence did some western diplomats in Salisbury conclude: 'Mugabe is streets ahead of his own people, and us.'

By and large, he's also managed to stay ahead of Joshua Nkomo, the man who some western observers have long since believed, could precipitate war. Nkomo took defeat in the election harder than anyone, for a while he genuinely could not believe he had lost. He accepted the home affairs ministry grudgingly, although it did give him a power base with its control of the police. Taunted by some of Mugabe's militants, like Enos Nkala, Nkomo has consistently refused to be drawn into open conflict with the government.

Nkomo knows that, if it came to war, his chances would be very slim. His well-trained army, Zipra, might take the towns for a while but they would face a much bigger army and now an air force as well. That sober prospect, more than anything, has made him compliant. So much so that when nine members of his party were arrested without his knowledge, indeed his permission as the minister responsible, Nkomo said: 'I feel like a china ornament sitting in the showcase.'

And what of the whites, whom Mugabe petitioned so strongly to stay? For most of his first year, Mugabe has been losing them at more than a thousand a month. At the end of 1980, the figures went higher. Many had waited for their children to complete the school year before going. Its more than he would have liked, the figure is comparable to the rate of exodus at the height of the war.

But there is more than a little consolation for him in the break-down of precisely who has gone and what gaps they leave in the ranks of skilled workers. Most of those who have gone have been retired people. In the first three months after independence, for example, Mugabe lost the following among the 'economically active' sectors of his people: 28 engineers, 21 electricians, 19 production super-intendents, eight male teachers, and three carpenters. He had a net gain during the same period of doctors: one more came than left.

There's no ground for complacency, as Mugabe knows all too well. The fact is, though, that he could hope to have a strong core of whites, about 80,000 of them, in five years time if the departure rate continues as it is today.

Arguably the greatest threat to Mugabe has been the

uneasy, fragile alliance of old friends, rivals and enemies that he put together last March.

Privately, Mugabe admitted that there would have to be casualties along the way. But he could never have known that Peter Walls and Edgar Tekere, two foes at extreme wings of his coalition, would figure among their number.

Walls' retirement in July last year came as no surprise. he had long since declared his intention to do so when he got the chance.

That he should retire and make it perfectly clear that he had such little faith and confidence in Mugabe's leadership was very damaging to the fragile Government alliance Mugabe was trying to strengthen. Walls, perhaps more than any other, was a symbol of Mugabe's determination to make the whites feel they could bury the past and stay on under him. If Walls, the arch-enemy, could live in peace with Mugabe, why not all the other whites?

Now Walls was gone, and in a manner calculated to hurt him. The general, it turned out when he was interviewed, had even tried to have the British government declare the election null and void amid stirring in his army of a coup against Mugabe back in March.

Not only had Mugabe lost the white most crucial to his policy of reconciliation, he now had militants in his party demanding retribution for 'this white treachery'. It was with a sad heart that Mugabe sacked and exiled Walls in September. It symbolised failure, maybe just with one individual, but an individual with undue influence on the whites.

In the wake of Walls, the Tekere case was enough to make the whites believe everything Walls had hinted, without ever saying, about the country's new rulers.

In itself, the murder of a white farmer did not shock anyone in the new Zimbabwe. There had been sporadic incidents like it ever since the election. But the fact that Tekere, cabinet minister, driving force in the party and one of Mugabe's erstwhile confidantes, was personally accused of leading the attack on a farmhouse ... well, it served only to confirm the worst suspicions fostered by the Smith regime throughout the years about 'racial slaughter' being the goal of the 'terrs'.

For Mugabe personally, it was a cruel blow and disappointment. Tekere, the man who had fled Zimbabwe with him in 1974, who had been with him through the year of uncertainty in Quelimane, who had loyally helped him to secure the leadership, would have to be tried for murder. It was to be humiliating, intensely embarrassing, not just for Tekere but also for Mugabe and his government.

'I don't look like a minister now,' said Tekere after his arrest. 'I've been fighting.'

Mugabe recognised the frustrations that Tekere was giving vent to: he also acknowledged that a growing number of party members felt he and his government were being just too moderate, too conciliatory, too practical and not radical enough.

Tekere's departure from the political scene, which most expected, would have undoubtedly strengthened Mugabe's control of his party. With Tekere out of the way, Mugabe could have spiked the guns of his troublesome left wing. Instead Tekere's acquittal made him even stronger, a greater threat to Mugabe – and a serious obstacle to his hopes of winning the confidence of the whites, who thought that Tekere had been given a licence to kill. The militant faction Tekere leads, his solid power base in his home province of Victoria and his reputation as an architect of the war always made him a possible heir apparent. Now, in the wake of the trial and acquittal, he was more than ever the man most likely to succeed.

If the men who fought the war expected pride of place in the revolution, if Nkomo wanted a greater role in government, if men like Tekere were impatient for radical change, then the hundreds of thousands of Africans who

215

voted Mugabe into power are also waiting for their rewards. The crisis of expectation among the country's seven million blacks is now arguably the greatest danger to Mugabe.

They expected immediate fruits, be it in higher wages or fuller employment. The revolution, after all, was made in their name. Even before Mugabe was installed as prime minister, black workers in Salisbury wielded a right to strike they had never had under Ian Smith. Now there is another battle on the shop-floor: not about wages or conditions, rather the right to represent the black worker. Mugabe's party, Zanu (PF), has been trying to assume control of the unions which up till now have been in the hands of those who worked with the previous regime, and supported it.

For the population at large Mugabe has not been able to produce instant panaceas. Indeed, his goals are too long-term for him even to wish to do so. In the days before he left Mozambique in January, he identified the awesome problems ahead. And the greatest was undoubtedly the re-settlement of the million people who had fled from their homes because of the war.

As Mugabe was taking over the wealthiest country of its size on the continent, the Salvation army was warning of the poverty ahead.

'If nothing is done about these people within a year ... there will be widespread starvation, disease, abandoned and orphaned children, alcohol addiction and violent crime affecting the entire population.'

Within a year a lot has been done. The 220,000 Zimbabweans who were in refugee camps in Mozambique, Zambia and Botswana have been repatriated. Hundreds of thousands more have been moved back to the tribal trustlands. Surprisingly, the first harvests of maize were good. They needed to be. Poverty remains a way of life in many areas of the country.

Mugabe says, with some justification, that it could be

so very different if the international community was prepared to put his fledgling revolution on its feet. Even before coming to power, he asked them for help, approaching more than 60 governments. The response has been a bitter disappointment. His calls for a 'mini Marshall plan' from the West have fallen on deaf ears.

Even those, like Britain, which promised aid have been held back by the state of their own economies. With Lord Soames as a strong advocate for his case, Mugabe had been pledged about 180 million dollars by Whitehall for reconstruction. But almost as quickly as the promise was made, it fell victim to Treasury constrictions in London. The initial help has been sent, but the rest will have to be spread out over three years because of Britain's recession.

The Americans, stymied by a Congress which is very cautious about the direction Mugabe might take, have produced about 30 million dollars. The West Germans, the Dutch, the Swedes have come forward but their pledges of aid have been limited to one year only. The combined response of the international community falls well short of Mugabe's needs. Indeed, its one of the ironies of a peace that both Britain and America have taken such pride in that the aid to support it falls well short even of the billion-dollar fund Dr Kissinger built into his first Anglo-American proposals back in 1976.

In the face of this, Mugabe has remained remarkably constant. Yes, he has hinted that Zimbabwe might become a one-party state: and yes, there have been suggestions that he might take over white-owned land. But Mugabe's visions of a one-party state is a far, far cry from dictatorship: and the land in question is only that which has been left to rot.

The man himself remains as committed as ever to the principles he outlined to the UN General Assembly when he made his debut there last September.

'When Zanu ascended to power we felt the moment

217

demanded of us a spirit of pragmatism, a spirit of realism, rather than that of emotionalism, a spirit of reconciliation and forgiveness rather than that of vindictiveness and retribution. We had to stand firm to achieve total peace rather than see our nation sink to the abyss of civil strife and continued war ... we had to embrace one another in the spirit of our one nationality, our common freedom and independence, our collective responsibility.'

About the same time Mugabe was asked how he, the psychopathic killer, the ogre, the terrorist of yesterday, had become the pragmatist, the moderate, the statesman of today. His reply was a testament to himself as man and politician. 'The change', he said, 'is not in me. I am not the one who has undergone a metamorphosis. The transformation really is taking place in the minds of those who once upon a time regarded me as an extremist, a murderer, a psychopathic killer ... they are the people who have had to adjust to the change. I have remained my constant self. What I was, I still am.'

Whether Mugabe can remain his constant self in the face of the crises that await him is an open question.

'His dilemma is that if he takes too much away from the whites they will leave.

'But if he gives too little to the blacks they will revolt.'

That, in the words of a British diplomat who had worked with him at Lancaster House and during the election, was the tightrope he had to tread after independence.

It is a tightrope he has to keep walking. A dilemma that cannot be solved until he has won the economic freedom that only the whites can give him.

No one should doubt his commitment, only whether he can buy himself enough time.

A Nurse's War

BY BRENDA McBRYDE
(illustrated)

IT TOOK COURAGE TO LIVE THROUGH IT – AND COURAGE TO WRITE ABOUT IT

Brenda McBryde's uniquely moving story began on the eve of
World War II when she enrolled as a trainee nurse at the
Royal Victoria Infirmary, Newcastle. The next six years saw
Sister McBryde nursing civilians through the Blitz,
volunteering for service in the Maxillo-Facial ('Max-Factor')
plastic surgery unit, joining the troops in the early days
following the D-Day landings, and serving in the Field
Hospitals in the front line of fighting. Then, as the war drew
to a close, she faced the greatest challenge of her career:
the restoration to health and sanity of Germany's
concentration camp victims.

'This book clutches the heart'
Cambridge Evening News

AUTOBIOGRAPHY   0 7221 5774 6   £1.25

PUT TO THE TEST

BY GEOFF BOYCOTT
(ILLUSTRATED)

ENGLAND'S No. 1 BATSMAN'S OWN COMPELLING STORY

PUT TO THE TEST is Geoff Boycott's fascinating story of the four-month Australian tour which resulted in England's triumphant retention of the Ashes.

Boycott discusses the extraordinary prelude to the tour; his feelings about the joint loss of the vice-captaincy of England and the captaincy of Yorkshire; the running battle with the Yorkshire Committee thousands of miles away and his ultimate decision to stay with the Club. And with cricket in turmoil after the Kerry Packer affair, he takes a hard look at the wider issues involving cricket and himself.

More than any other player in the history of the game, Boycott vividly conveys what it really feels like to be out in the middle, hour by hour, session by session. His frankness and candour in this personal account make **PUT TO THE TEST** a compelling read.

AUTOBIOGRAPHY   0 7221 1791 4   £1.25

A selection of bestsellers from **SPHERE**

FICTION

STEPPING	Nancy Thayer	£1.25 ☐
THE GRAIL WAR	Richard Monaco	£1.75 ☐
UNHOLY CHILD	Catherine Breslin	£1.75 ☐
TO LOVE AGAIN	Danielle Steel	£1.25 ☐
THE ELDORADO NETWORK	Derek Robinson	£1.50 ☐

FILM AND TV TIE-INS

LLOYD GEORGE	David Benedictus	£1.25 ☐
THE EMPIRE STRIKES BACK	Donald F. Glut	£1.00 ☐
CLOSE ENCOUNTERS OF THE THIRD KIND	Steven Spielberg	85p ☐
BUCK ROGERS IN THE 25TH CENTURY	Addison E. Steele	95p ☐
BUCK ROGERS 2: THAT MAN ON BETA	Addison E. Steele	95p ☐

NON-FICTION

A MATTER OF LIFE	R. Edwards & P. Steptoe	£1.50 ☐
SUPERLEARNING	Sheila Ostrander & Lynn Schroeder with Nancy Ostrander	£1.75 ☐
SPACE	Martin Ince	£1.50 ☐
MENACE: The Life and Death of the Tirpitz	Ludovic Kennedy	£1.25 ☐

All Sphere books are available at your local bookshop or newsagent, or can be ordered direct from the publisher. Just tick the titles you want and fill in the form below.

Name _____

Address _____

_____

Write to Sphere Books, Cash Sales Department, P.O. Box 11, Falmouth, Cornwall TR10 9EN

Please enclose cheque or postal order to the value of the cover price plus:

UK: 25p for the first book plus 12p per copy for each additional book ordered to a maximum charge of £1.05.

OVERSEAS: 40p for the first book and 12p for each additional book.

BFPO & EIRE: 25p for the first book plus 10p per copy for the next 8 books, thereafter 5p per book.

Sphere Books reserve the right to show new retail prices on covers which may differ from those previously advertised in the text or elsewhere, and to increase postal rates in accordance with the PO.